Bread, Butter, and Bacon: Hungry for Success

The Art of Making a Livelihood

Stevan Pirkovic

Bread, Butter, and Bacon: Hungry for Success

The Art of Making a Livelihood

For information, contact:

Stevan Pirkovic

(810) 356-5116

Stevan@Pirkovic.com

Cover design by Stevan Pirkovic

Cover images courtesy of Google Free Images

Book edited and designed by Joni Wilson

ISBN: 978-0-9961479-0-3

First Edition: April 2015

Contents

Acknowledgments

This is the section of the book where I thank everyone who helped me publish my ideas. A big thanks to Joni Wilson and the three little letters that can move mountains...

1. ..M

2. I

3. .....H

4. ....

5. ....

6. ....

7. ....

8. ....

9. ....

10. ....

11. ....

12. ....

13. ....

14. ....

15. ....MAKE IT HAPPEN!

What's your
bread and butter?

How do you
bring home the bacon?

1

My Story

I've been fooled. Up until now, my whole life has been based on one huge delusion. The essence of everything I've done has stemmed from one little lie. Want me to let you in on a secret? You've been told this lie too. Now you're probably thinking, *what is this grand illusion?*

Well, it's something you've been told countless times while you were growing up. "Work hard in high school, get into a good college, get a degree, get a job, and live happily ever after." Like many people, I grew up hearing this story repeatedly, eventually to the point where I believed it to be an unquestionable truth. But the sky is always blue, until it's not. And how can you not believe in an idea that gets lectured to you every day?

Now what I actually encountered didn't quite turn out like a picture-perfect blue sky. The skies in my journey were slightly gray and cloudy at times, but they've just began to break and let in the amazing blue-orange glow of a beautiful, crisp, clear sunset, and that's where this journey beings.

I went through the normal education regimen of elementary school, high school, and college. At each stage, like many children, I fought it tooth and nail. Looking back, I wish I had embraced school and the idea of education more. But I had no craving for it.

Back then, I would have rather played video games, gone to an amusement park, or watched a movie—anything but learning.

I wasn't one to sit in a room all day and listen to someone lecture and drone on about something I had no interest in. I was more inclined to learn on my own, and I did. By the time I reached college, I found that I absorbed more information when I was reading or studying by myself.

While I learned better on my own, I also took longer than most kids to finish my work. I found myself in countless situations where I was rushing against deadlines for homework and final papers. It took me so long to get things done, because I was easily distracted when I was trying to study.

Looking back at the endless hours I spent doing everything except my schoolwork and all those near-deadline misses, I think I probably had Attention Deficit Disorder (ADD), because I would find myself distracted all the time. And not just slightly distracted, I mean sidetracked for hours on end. But I never gave it any thought in terms of medical attention. I just thought I was procrastinating and constantly preoccupied in class.

Eventually I graduated from college. The concept of making a livelihood really didn't hit me until I started working at my third job after college. After I graduated, I was just looking for work, any work, just something to pay the bills. But I knew this wasn't a long-term solution. Because, like many college graduates, I was working and doing things that I had no interest in—jobs that I really didn't study for or train for while in college. And this really impacted my outlook on life. Doing a job just to do it is not a great way to make a living. Especially so if you are not even using your skills or what you've learned.

So there I was at work, sitting at a desk on a hot, summer day in August, aimlessly staring into a computer monitor. With a blank expression on my face, I could not move my eyes off the screen. I was stuck like a splotch of peanut butter on a piece of bread.

I had so many thoughts going through my head that I couldn't keep track of them. I felt like I was in the middle of a tornado, helplessly trying to grab my belongings as they were being blown into the abyss.

I broke free from my trance, and I managed to open my email. I started writing an email to myself. The subject line was just one word, *"Career."* I had grown to a point in my life where I thought I knew myself fairly well. So I started to type a list of things that I knew I was good at. I thought that if I could just figure out where I'd fit in, then I could figure out what to do with my life.

But at the ripe age of 25, I still really didn't know what my passions were. What did I really want to do with my life? I knew that I was just working at a job as an administrative assistant. Could I have turned that into a career? There is nothing wrong with that profession, and I sure could have. It was just that I couldn't bring myself to do it, day in and day out—not if I could change it.

It was a good idea, and it was the *"safe option,"* but realistically following through with it would have been pure torture for me. Can you imagine getting up every day and dreading going to work? I'm sure many people feel like this. And it was at this point I realized that I was doing something wrong. How could others around me seem as if they enjoyed the work? Why did some of my relatives and friends seem to *"have it figured out"*? If they could, then I could too.

I continued to make a list of things that I was good at. And then I noticed that I could group my list into categories. A lot of things were similar in one way or another, so it made sense to group them. I ended up making three categories, each with about five to six things I was good at. I didn't know what I was going to do with this list, but I knew I just had to get it out of my head and onto the twenty-first century version of a piece of paper, an email on my phone.

Here's a copy of the email I sent to myself.

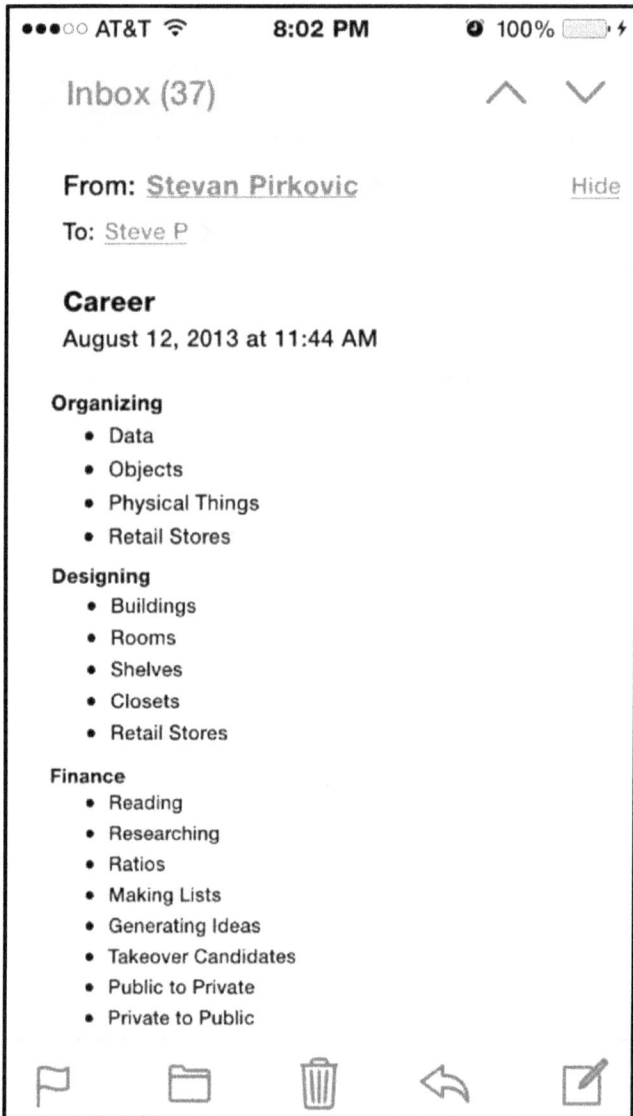

●●●○○ AT&T 📶   8:02 PM   ⏺ 100% ⬛⬛⬛ ⚡

Inbox (37)   ⌃ ⌄

From: <u>Stevan Pirkovic</u>   Hide

To: <u>Steve P</u>

Career
August 12, 2013 at 11:44 AM

Organizing
- Data
- Objects
- Physical Things
- Retail Stores

Designing
- Buildings
- Rooms
- Shelves
- Closets
- Retail Stores

Finance
- Reading
- Researching
- Ratios
- Making Lists
- Generating Ideas
- Takeover Candidates
- Public to Private
- Private to Public

⚑   🗁   🗑   ↩   ✎

I kept the descriptions fairly vague. However, you'll notice that I have a knack for organizing. I love putting things in order, whether it's data on a spreadsheet or food in a pantry. I first realized this when I briefly worked as a stock boy at a small grocery store. I loved stacking and filling shelves with boxes and cans of food. I turned out to be great at it. I was quick, creative, and not afraid of organizing even the biggest of messes. Ever since then, I've been fascinated with grocery stores, retail stores, gas stations, and even my own kitchen.

But I realized that my fascination with organization really didn't translate into a readily obtainable degree at college. So it probably won't surprise you that I double-majored in economics and business administration, and I minored in political science. I slowly turned my obsession for organization into more marketable skills within the fields of finance and accounting.

So what did this email message do for me? It really made the point that I should focus on finding work around these concepts and fields. While I'm still searching for the "right job" and learning my "passions," I think I'm on the right track. And I'm reminded of a famous saying by the Chinese philosopher and teacher, Confucius.

> *"Choose a job you love, and*
> *you will never have to work a day in your life."*

> —Confucius

This saying is really enlightening. But I found that you shouldn't just arbitrarily choose your job. That, in itself, is a losing battle. If you were to take Confucius quite literally, then everyone would want to be, "movie stars," "beer taste testers," or "professional poker players." But we all know that just isn't the reality. Sure, these are jobs people might love doing, but not everyone has the ability or skills for them. And the truth is, someone has to do those jobs. Someone has to taste-test beer and star in movies.

And it's the people with certain skill sets who are doing those jobs. It's people who probably have a passion for what they do and make a livelihood out of it.

And what I discovered is that there is more than meets the eye when you're looking for a job. This idea is what led me to continue writing my thoughts about my list. I eventually started to write this book about how to actually make a livelihood.

I hope my story has captured your curiosity. I certainly was amazed at the mountains of literature, books, and videos in the world about "success" and "how to be your own boss." But after reviewing hundreds of these, I really didn't find anything that had practical real-life applications or anything that explained how to make a livelihood.

I did what I do best. I laid out the entire concept and started mapping. I believe what I have written is an excellent guide on how to figure out how to make your livelihood. I hope this helps you, as much as it's helped me.

2

Introduction

How many times have you heard someone say they don't know what they want to do with their life? As I was growing up, I heard this from many people, young and old, at different stages; however, I always knew that everyone had to do something. After high school, I saw friends and colleagues venturing off into life— some went to college, some were employed in far-flung fields of work, and some worked in more traditional jobs. I could clearly see that some people had their acts together, while others hadn't the slightest clue.

How does everyone end up in their individual situations? Why do some people know exactly what they want to study in college, while others go to college to *"find themselves"?* How come some people can find *"their calling"* or *"their passion,"* while others struggle to find theirs? Why do some people find *"success"* in working for themselves, being self-employed, while others *"succeed"* in working for an organization, as an employee?

Most people will immediately say that the answers to these questions are found in *"chance," "fate,"* or *"God,"* depending on their religious views. People often use the phrase, *"You have to play the hand you were dealt,"* to describe how they found their job, or how they figured out how to make their living. I can even attest to the notion that *"chance"* plays a role in finding a livelihood, because I've experienced it firsthand in finding my job. While it's true to some extent, I don't believe it's the whole story.

However, I believe that no matter what your religious views are or what you believe about the *"universe,"* there is an art behind making your livelihood. It's an art that if studied and mastered can help you find your way through life and help you make your *"bread and butter"* and *"bring home the bacon."*

While everyone's situation is different, I believe most people can benefit from understanding the art behind making a livelihood. That is to say, some people will find that this book does not apply to them. In that case, I believe they would still benefit from understanding where everyone else in their lives is coming from. And the opposite is also true. Some people will find that this book sheds new light on how to make a livelihood and establishes a useful framework on how to think about life.

Personally, I wish that someone had explained this framework and these ideas to me when I was younger and growing up. But, as with most things in life, I learned about this *"the hard way."* I am of the type who learns from reading, then doing. I'm the guy who will read the owner's manual to figure out how to use his iPhone. That is to say, I still enjoy learning from experience. It's just that whenever possible, I'd like to learn from the experience of others. I'll be the first to tell you that the best way to learn a job at work is to watch someone else do it—shadow them. For me, that is how I learned, working my way up in my job.

But what about life lessons, like making a livelihood in the first place? It's true that the best lessons in life are taught when you set out to try something for yourself and fail; I believe that this is the ultimate learning tool. However, history is full of lessons and stories from people who've come before us and have passed down their knowledge. So why not take advantage of this history? If not for the simple tradition, then for the value in knowing that someone tried something and wrote about how it succeeded or how it failed. I'm reminded of a few quotes about learning from experience.

> *"Only a fool learns from his own mistakes.*
> *The wise man learns from the mistakes of others."*
> —Otto von Bismarck

> *"All men make mistakes,*
> *but only wise men learn from their mistakes."*
> —Winston Churchill

> *"Learn from the mistakes of others.*
> *You can't live long enough to make them all yourself."*
> —Eleanor Roosevelt

We all engage in this **"experience gathering."** This is what you're doing when you read a news article or learn how to install your newest kitchen appliance, or other do-it-yourself (DIY) projects. You are either reading, watching, or listening about the experiences of someone else in an attempt to learn something new to prepare for your own endeavors.

One way to learn from others is to be around people. In his famous book, **The Black Swan: The Impact of the Highly Improbable,** author Nassim Nicholas Taleb suggests that we can learn from the **"mistakes of others"** by being socially outgoing. Vincent Kaminski, former managing director for research at the failed energy firm Enron, even echoes this idea, saying that by being able to "**socialize a lot,**" we can learn from people's stories and past experiences.

However, while the technique of **"networking"** and **"socialization"** can broaden your experience, it's not the only way we learn from others. Another way is by reading. Learning from experience is also like learning from reading, particularly when it comes to concepts and ideas. I find it best to read about the idea, because there is really no practical way for someone to show you an abstract concept or idea other than attempting to do so with pictures, words, or video.

While learning from experience has helped me master tasks that make me successful at work, I have not found it helpful for learning concepts. Some might like having a book or subject lectured to them by someone else, while others might like to learn on their own. In either case, the same outcome is achieved. Learning something that is new to you, from someone else who has experienced the subject firsthand. Whether it's presented in a book, on a whiteboard, or in a PowerPoint presentation, you are gathering information about the concept, the idea, or learning from someone else's experience.

I wrote this book as a guide with examples to showcase different people's lives and their stories. I start with what I call the *"Tri-Skills Framework"* in Chapter 3. This framework then feeds into the two-skill dichotomy, called *"STEML vs. PADS"* covered in Chapter 4. Then I explore the four possible combinations, or what I call *"The Four Quadrants,"* of the Tri-Skills Framework and STEML vs. PADS dichotomy in Chapter 5.

In Chapters 6 through 9, I provide examples of individuals I believe have made successful livelihoods. This is done by presenting interviews or speeches they've given, and I provide my commentary. To conclude the book, I offer some *"Final Thoughts"* in Chapter 10 to send you on your journey to finding your livelihood.

I'm confident that my framework and the relevant examples will show you how to successfully create a livelihood for yourself and allow you to *"bring home the bacon."*

3

Tri-Skills Framework

It all comes down to skills. What are you good at? The key to unlocking your livelihood starts with a basic understanding of economics, capitalism, and human behavior. To many people, these subjects are as clear as muddy water. But I didn't set out to write a book about these cryptic subjects, rather I'm trying to explain them in a way that anyone who is looking for a livelihood can understand these ideas.

Forgoing a history lesson on economics, I believe we can all agree on the idea that life revolves around a series of transactions. Person A has something Person B wants, and Person B will pay Person A for their good or service. We see this every day of every month of every year.

I assume most readers pay their electric bills every month. The power company has something we all want—and let's face it, something we all need—electricity. I on my own do not have the resources to provide electricity for my house. Instead of building a power plant, which I know nothing about, I essentially subcontract my electricity needs to a power company that specializes in selling electricity to anyone who pays for it.

The power company has a special skill; it knows how to make electricity and how to get it from a power plant 100 miles away right into your house, through your walls, and into your bedroom lamp. Like I mentioned, I have no idea how to even start to create a set-up like this to provide electricity on my own, and because this is not my skill, I gladly pay the power company to do this for me.

Now you might ask yourself, *"Well, this is good and all, but where do I get money and resources to even pay the power company for electricity?* The answer is simple: You make money with your skills. You as an individual have your own set of skills. As we'll discuss in the next chapter, some people know their natural abilities and skills from the beginning at a young age, while others find their skills later in life or need training and education to learn or master a skill.

But let's assume, for now, that you already know what your skill is at this point in time. Let's say that you are a talented chef at a fancy five-star restaurant. You earn money and make your livelihood from cooking at a restaurant. This is your specialty; it's your skill. So when you need electricity for your house to make a pot of coffee and to have lights to brighten your room at night, you turn to the power company to buy your electricity. That's the smart thing to do. It's more beneficial and efficient for you to simply pay someone else to do this for you, because you're a chef.

You have no idea how to bring electricity to your house and most likely don't have time to figure how to do it. It would be a gigantic waste of time, for example, if you figured out a way to get a loan to build a power plant or install wind turbines to provide your house with electricity. The time and effort that you would need to spend on a project like that, far outweighs any benefits you would realistically reap. It is smarter to focus on your skills and pay others for theirs. You need to **delegate**, just like you would when you see a doctor for your ailment or a car mechanic for your car trouble.

Can you change the oil in your car? Sure, but you'd first need to know how to do it. You need to know the mechanics of changing the oil, then you'd need the resources and time to change the oil, and finally you need to actually want to get down and dirty and change the oil yourself. Just like America's number one independent financial advisor, Ric Edelman says, **"You need competency, capability, and desirability"** to actually do something you're not well versed in. It's a balancing act, and there are trade-offs you need to consider.

The minute you start to want to do everything yourself, you begin a losing battle. Just like the founder of a company who can't let go, you'll be pulling your hair out over the mounting piles of tasks that you could easily pay someone else to do for you. Especially as a corporate executive officer (CEO) or manager, you want to spend your time planning a larger strategy for your organization; you don't want to focus your time on neverending tasks, because, **"no one else knows how I want it done."**

You don't want to end up being a Jack or Jill of all trades and master of nothing. I quickly realized this when I wrote that email to myself at work on that hot August day. The organization I worked for was pushing everyone to do increasingly more tasks beyond their normal daily scope of work. The job descriptions we started with weren't a reflection of the job we ended up doing.

And, unfortunately, more companies engage in this behavior in an attempt to reduce costs and increase margins. Training employees to be versed in multiple systems or tasks, often called **"cross-training,"** goes against the grain of specialization. It's not a natural fit for most people, and it creates an unhealthy environment full of barriers to task completion, knowledge hoarding, and inconsistency. Often times when an organization starts down this path, it tries to do more with less, and ends up overburdening the few employees it has left, which ironically doesn't help the margins and ultimately hurts the bottom lines. On the flip side, companies and organizations that embrace the natural tendencies of specialization and collaboration are often the trendsetters, innovators, and the people who lead in their markets.

World-renowned author Shane Parrish, from the famous blog Farnam Street, eloquently sums up this dichotomy by pointing to famous venture capitalist Ben Horowitz's book, ***The Hard Thing About Hard Things: Building a Business When There Are No Easy Answers,*** in which Horowitz writes,

> *"In good organizations, people can focus on their work and have confidence that if they get their work done, good things will happen for both the company and them personally . . . In a poor organization, on the other hand, people spend much of their time fighting organizational boundaries, infighting, and broken processes. They are not even clear on what their jobs are, so there is no way to know if they are getting the job done or not"* (101).

This basic idea of specialization and skills is the backbone of the economy, as it exists today. Your mission is to find where you best fit and what your skills are. This is easier said than done.

However, before I get into finding your skills, we need to recognize the importance of the different avenues that skill utilization can take in relation to making a livelihood.

The Tri-Skills Framework breaks down how skills are used in making a livelihood. It's tough enough finding or developing your skill. Before you start on that path, you need to know that even if you obtain a marketable skill, it might not necessarily result in the optimal livelihood you originally sought.

In the words of Ben Carpenter and his book, ***The Bigs: The Secrets Nobody Tells Students and Young Professionals about How to Find a Great Job, Do a Great Job, Be a Leader, Start a Business, Stay Out of Trouble, and Live A Happy Life,*** you will best be served by finding out what you are good at doing. This might not necessarily be the thing that you are passionate about. Your skills and passions can be different. This is the major dilemma in making a livelihood. Your skills and passions might be two diverse things, as is the case with most people. In a perfect world, your skills and passions would be aligned.

Two things I hear often from job-seeking young adults are, ***"Do you like your job?"*** or ***"I can't find a job doing what I like."*** The key to making a livelihood is to align your skills, natural or learned, with your passions and goals. It's no secret that many people don't like their jobs, because it's a job.

Let's say on the basic level that you essentially have nothing—no skills, no money, no resources, etc. You do have one thing that others will pay you for, and that is your time and labor. You can always trade these for money, doing almost anything you can get others to pay you to do, such as working as a cashier, mowing lawns, laying tile floors, painting walls, etc.

But these ***"jobs"*** or tasks are not usually what most people are passionate about and not anyone's ideal goal in life. That's not to say they can't be your passion; they certainly can. But over the course of my life, I have rarely met anyone who genuinely says that they ***"love"*** the job they do for a living. These individuals are people who are truly making a livelihood for themselves and love what they do and do what they love.

However, most people with ***"jobs"*** when asked if they like what they do, usually say they do. It's like a gut reaction, an instant reflex. Just like when someone says to you, ***"Good morning, how are you doing?"*** Everyone, almost 99 percent of the time, will reply with, ***"Excellent, how about you?"*** or ***"Doing well!"*** It's human nature; we want to project that we're doing better than others or at least offer that perception. And the same goes for people and their ***"jobs."***

When most people say they like their job, what they're actually saying is that they can survive and withstand getting up every day doing something they don't like or have no interest in doing. Over time perhaps, people might get so accustomed to doing their ***"job"*** that they trick themselves into actually thinking they really like it. At that point, they've essentially become a robot. And no one I've met ever aspired to be a robot, except that weird kid I met one day at the playground in elementary school. Although, I think he's now an electrical engineer, so I think it's safe to say he's found his passion for robots, or close to it.

Most people work a job that they don't enjoy, just to pay their bills, so they can continue living to keep paying their bills, to keep working at a job that they don't like. If that last sentence sounds familiar, it is because world-renowned philosopher and often-quoted writer Alan Watts said the same thing more than fifty years ago, and it's still true today.

Most people will accept this as a fact and think no further beyond this idea. This concept is, in fact, the first part of the Tri-Skills Framework. The image on the next page explains where all three parts are in relation to each other. The following page explains each component in detail.

Tri-Skills Framework

ALIGNMENT

Skills = Passions + Goals

Your skills match your passions & goals

Earning a True Livelihood

MISALIGNMENT

Skills ≠ Passions + Goals

Your skills don't match your passions & goals

You earn a living to fund your passions

BORDERLINE

You have no passions or goals OR

No need for skills to reach your goals OR

Unable to find or learn a skill

Tri-Skills Framework

1. Alignment

- You discover your skill.

- You are either born with it or learn it via schooling.

- You obtain further education or training to enhance it.

- You also discover that this is your passion.

- Your livelihood is your passion and vice-versa.

2. Misalignment

- You aren't necessarily born with a marketable skill.

- You search the options of ***"best fits"*** and decide on a skill.

- You attend school or training to learn and master your chosen skill.

- You make your livelihood from your skill to fund your passions.

- Your skills and passions are misaligned, but you are able to achieve a balance of sorts between your work and your passions.

- This is why jobs offer vacations, get-a-ways, "it's five o'clock somewhere," trips and experiences, to allow you time for your passions.

3. Borderline

(Well-off or the worst possible situation imaginable)

- You are born with a skill but do not (*or are unable to*) use it to make a livelihood.

- You have enough resources to pursue and achieve your passions without making a livelihood with your skills.

- You don't have a skill, but also do not require a skill to make your livelihood.

- You are unable to learn a skill to achieve your passions.

- You have passions but no way of achieving them due to lack of skills.

Let's explain each part of the framework with a few examples. In the following examples, I'll use the idea of someone who first discovers their skill, then someone who learns their skill, and then finally someone who is borderline.

Alignment

For example, let's say you discover, as a young child, that you have the uncanny ability to build wooden birdhouses. It comes to you so naturally. Measuring and cutting wood is like breathing air; you don't think twice about it. You can build several birdhouses in one day. You make so many birdhouses that you end up loving what you do.

You eventually start holding seminars about birdhouses in your neighborhood. You start a YouTube channel and quickly gain thousands of followers. A few companies decide to sponsor you, and you now spend six months out of the year touring the world making appearances and holding seminars.

This has become your passion. You love showing people the magic and wonder of birdhouses and how they help birds. In this case, your skills are aligned with your passions.

Misalignment

For example, let's say you are a young adult, trying to figure out what to do for the rest of your life. You have taken several aptitude tests and job-shadowed with several companies while in high school, but you have yet to find something that you are good at—and, more important, something you like to do. The only thing that seemingly gives you enjoyment and that you are passionate about is your dog.

You go everywhere with your dog and spend a lot of time with your dog. But you can't figure out how to take your passion for your dog and make a livelihood out of it. One afternoon, you are browsing your local newspaper and read an article about the booming business of handmade birdhouses. This gets your attention, and you decide to give it a try. You end up being a natural at building birdhouses. You soon become the best birdhouse maker in the entire state. People come from all over to buy your birdhouses.

You eventually start holding seminars about birdhouses in your neighborhood. You start a YouTube channel and quickly gain thousands of followers. You then begin traveling around the world hosting seminars and making appearances about how to build the perfect birdhouse.

This is a conflict for you, because you really miss being with your dog. But the success your skill has brought you, now allows you to take significant time away from the birdhouse industry to spend with your dog. You only occasionally delve into your birdhouses but you can afford to spend quality time with your dog. In this case, your skills are misaligned with your passion. You build birdhouses, so you can acquire resources to spend time with your dog.

Borderline

For example, let's say you are born into a wealthy family. You notice early on that you have a natural ability to build birdhouses. You build birdhouses occasionally; however, you do not rely on this as your livelihood, because you have other, larger, passive sources of income.

Or consider the following: let's say that you have no wealth or no natural skills. You attempt to learn a skill in order to make a livelihood, but you are unable to learn anything that is marketable.

You also have a passion for building birdhouses. But you are not very good at it. You could never actually build a fully functional birdhouse, but it is your passion, even though you cannot make a livelihood out of it.

You find yourself needing to provide for your family and you obtain a service industry livelihood as a custodian. This livelihood does not require any particular skill, however, it allows you to provide for your family and spend any leftover resources on your passion.

4

STEML vs. PADS

So now that we've covered how skills come into play within the framework of making a livelihood, let's break down the two major skill types. Skills can fall into two major categories—STEML and PADS. These can be further assigned into four different scenarios or quadrants, which we will cover in the next chapter.

When it's all said and done, skills are skills. Either you have found your skill, or you haven't yet. If you've found it, then focus on it and become a master at it. If you haven't found it, then you might want to consider learning a skill in the meantime and becoming a master at it.

STEML is an abbreviation for science, technology, engineering, math, and law. PADS is an abbreviation for persuasion, art, design, and sales. While it's difficult to make a clear and concise distinction among skills in general, I think it's safe to crack the egg right down the middle and say that for the most part skills fall into one of these two camps. The image below explains the distinction between both categories.

PADS vs. STEML

PADS

Persuasion | Art | Design |Sales

- Soft sciences / skills
- Practical skill and expertise
- Implicit knowledge
- Selling goods and services (made by others or yourself)
- Convince someone to exchange their money for your good or service
- Selling a better mousetrap
- People skills and networking
- A new customer is born every minute

Both PADS and STEML

Skills can be born-with and/or acquired/learned; Can attend school/college/university for training

STEML

Science | Technology | Engineering | Math | Law

- Hard sciences / skills
- Theoretical and abstract
- Explicit knowledge
- Exchange & disseminate knowledge & ideas
- Demonstrates skills via production, projects, cases or on-going studies
- Constant testing of knowledge through exams, papers, projects, dissertations, or state & federal licensing, etc.

Often times both of these skill sets go hand in hand. That's not to say that someone absolutely needs both skill sets. It's just beneficial to know how to use both types in making a livelihood. For now, let's focus on each individual skill set to see how they provide the tools to make a livelihood.

Let's start with PADS. It's been said by many people that if you want to be successful and make a livelihood you need to *"sell."* And that is what PADS is all about. Since the beginning of time, the ability to convince others to do something for your benefit or exchange their resources for yours has been critical in people's success.

Some people seem to be born with this ability, and for others it might develop naturally. People might describe a PADS-oriented individual as *"a people person"* or *"outgoing."* Other people might pick this skill up over time or learn it as they mature. People with this skill also tend to be creative and often think *"outside the box."*

The idea of PADS is that if you don't have a firm grasp or understanding of some of the *"hard sciences"* or *"traditional fields,"* then you must, for the sake of making a meaningful livelihood, learn how to *"sell."* Now this isn't limited to literally being a door-to-door salesperson. It means that if you don't have knowledge to sell, or you don't want to sell your time/labor, then you need to sell something that someone else made.

PADS occupations can often be found in the *"service sector"* or *"service industry."* For example, on the extreme end, a PADS-oriented individual might be an insurance salesperson, selling policies to customers most likely in exchange for a commission and an hourly wage or salary. On the opposite end, a PADS-oriented individual might be a hairstylist who works either in a salon or on their own, who treats and styles customers' hair. The stylists need to *"sell"* their brand and their personality. The stylist's customers don't get their hair cut because of the salon's name; they get their hair cut because of the stylist giving them the haircut. The relationship with the stylist is what the customer is actually buying.

This subtle touch of PADS is found everywhere and with anyone making their livelihood in a PADS fields. Just think about all the places you go or that you shop. The name of the store or company might draw you in, but it's the people providing the service who keep you coming back—they build that relationship with you. The service providers are selling their brand to you. They take the time to talk to you and get to know you. This technique is a must-have skill for anyone in PADS, from a real estate agent, to a car salesman, to an artist.

PADS is also an art form. In between both extreme ends, an insurance salesperson on one end, and a hair stylist on the other, PADS also resonates with the creative and talented in the middle. Along with selling goods or services offered by others or yourself, PADS also encompasses the entertainment world. This includes everything from musicians, magicians, athletes, actors, and any other form of media you can think of.

For example, take someone who discovers at a young age that they have a talent and skill for *"art."* People notice that this young individual is talented. If this young person can match his passion with their *"art"* skills, then he should pursue it. But how does this young person make a livelihood with *"art"*? The answer lies in the notion that he needs to build his brand and expand his network.

The young person's *"art"* skill will only make them a living, if they can convince someone else to trade the *"art"* for financial resources. As such, we often recognize and remember the most famous artists, athletes, and musicians. These individuals, with a little luck, are able to promote and convince others that they are worth a listen or the price of admission.

"Beauty is in the eye of the beholder," as the famous saying goes. The most popular artist, athlete or musician might not necessarily be the *"best"* in terms of quality or performance. This is why, for example, *"teen pop"* or *"bubble gum"* music becomes popular and makes the artist behind the addicting songs a nice livelihood. These songs often have no substance of any significance behind their lyrics compared to more serious and passionate music, yet people seem to enjoy it. As long as individuals have the power of persuasion and are convincing enough, they can sell anything to anyone, from insurance, to haircuts, and even music.

So if PADS is just about the pure ability to *"sell,"* then what is STEML about? Recall that I'm defining STEML as an abbreviation for science, technology, engineering, math, and law. This is slightly different from the traditional STEM category, which excludes law from its acronym. I specifically chose to include law in this category, because I believe it is *"hard science,"* and, like other sciences, it requires vast memorization and continuous learning and updating.

This might seem like a conflicting idea, because law by its nature requires its operators to be versed in *"selling."* But this is an idea we often see portrayed in popular media in which lawyers are "ambulance chasers." While there is a large segment of people who practice law who are trial lawyers, the broader idea of law is more suited for the STEM category. While trial lawyers and the entire concept of the judicial system lie in the skill of being able to convince the judge or jury, I still think that lawyers need to have a knowledge base of written law, no matter how little, in order to effectively make a livelihood in the legal field.

But with that said, the idea of STEM has proliferated among higher education officials and academics for a long time. This idea basically advocates that increased importance should be placed on the subjects and fields of science, technology, engineering, and mathematics. These fields are often referred to as the *"hard sciences"* or *"hard skills."*

These are *"hard"* as opposed to *"soft,"* because people in the STEM fields are largely dealing with ideas and concepts and the interactions of these ideas with other ideas and concepts. While there is some *"soft selling"* in STEM, it is more often between *"things"* rather than between people, like in PADS.

On the extreme end, someone in a STEML field is the complete opposite of someone in a PADS field. A STEML-oriented person might not have any people skills or social skills. Their strong suit is in their knowledge and problem-solving abilities. STEMLs make their livelihoods by trading their knowledge for financial resources. In some cases, STEMLs might have to sell their knowledge, but often times the audience is captive, and it might be considered by some as an *"easy sell."*

For example, let's say a young person is a "bookworm" growing up, and they love reading and thinking about boats and ships that sail the sea. They don't have a lot of people skills, and, for the most part, they fly under the radar. However, they find an opportunity to turn their passion for boats and ships into a skill.

While at college, they enroll in a naval architecture and marine engineering program. There they learn all sorts of knowledge about ship engineering and boat design. They thoroughly enjoy their education and soon graduate. After graduation, the young adult has a STEML skill set she can use while pursuing her passions (alignment). She is soon hired by a top naval engineering company to design ships and vessels for offshore oil exploration.

In this case, the young person really didn't have to sell her skills in order to make a livelihood, like a PADS-oriented individual would have to. It's safe to say that the labor pool of naval engineers is extremely small compared to the pool of hair stylists and insurance salespeople. Numerically speaking, there is a higher probability of someone who has a specialized skill, such as naval engineering, being able to make a livelihood compared to someone who has yet to find their skill or simply is in any of the PADS fields. The barriers to entry are also far higher in the naval engineering field compared to the sales industry.

The demand of naval and marine engineering far outpaces the supply of the available talent, which is why the probability of success is so high. Whereas the supply of PADS talent is far more than the demand for it, which is why there is a plethora of sales, marketing, and business-development opportunities.

5

The Four Quadrants

Before I begin this chapter, here are just a few notes. This is one of the longer chapters, as it ties in the framework with the PADS and STEML dichotomy. Later in the chapter, I'll use the following symbol, *"# # #,"* to help create breaks between different sections.

As described in the previous chapter, the idea of STEM has been proliferated among higher education officials and academics for a long time. This idea basically advocates that increased importance be placed on the subjects and fields of science, technology, engineering, and mathematics. To recap, these fields are often referred to as the *"hard sciences"* or *"hard skills."*

Naturally, when there is a group of people advocating for the acceptance of one or multiple fields of study over another, there are bound to be clashes. Fields such as art, design, humanities, and philosophy have their own advocates and often spar with STEM supporters, because they advocate the importance of *"softer skills."* And, in my opinion, what is life, truly, without art? Life should not be all *"black and white"* and *"linear 1+1=2."* There needs to be some variety.

However, as I will demonstrate in the following pages, the distinction between both STEML and PADS can be set-up in a four-quadrant framework. Naturally, the first two quadrants are PADS and STEML, respectively. These two upper quadrants represent the idea that someone solely has either PADS or STEML skills.

The lower quadrants represent the combination and the opposite of the upper quadrants. The combination of both PADS and STEML skill sets is what I call a *"deadly combination."* This makes up the third quadrant. Any individual is not limited to learning either PADS or STEML separately. There are many instances where someone can possess both skill sets.

The probability of successfully making a livelihood is the highest in this quadrant. When someone is able to implement both skill sets in their livelihood then they are a *"complete package."* Another instance where *"deadly combinations"* might often arise is in organizations or companies. Often times, STEML founders or inventors team up with PADS managers and salespeople to get their inventions or products to the market.

And finally, the fourth quadrant is what I call *"none of the above."* Reminiscent of the fictional political party started by Monty Brewster in the movie, *Brewster's Millions,* starring world-renowned actors Richard Pryor and John Candy, this quadrant represents the outliers to this framework and the various situations where individuals might not have a need for or are unable to learn either PADS or STEML skills.

The image on the next page shows the four quadrants. The next two pages explain the various ways in which PADS and STEML skills are utilized in each quadrant.

Livelihood's Four Quadrants

PADS	STEML
PADS + STEML	**None of the Above**

Stevan Pirkovic © 2015

Livelihood's Four Quadrants (1 of 2)

PADS ONLY

Based on socially outgoing people. Generally someone who is convincing and persuading (*"people skills"* and *"networking"*). Sells goods and services for larger organizations. No formal educational training is required. People sometimes enter fields like *"communications and marketing"* or earn an *"MBA"* or *"business"* degree for sales. *Can work individually or as a part of a larger organization.* Examples:

- Pharmaceutical Sales
- Copy Machine Sales
- Car Sales
- Cell Phone Sales
- Real Estate Sales
- Financial Services Sales
- Insurance Sales
- Healthcare Sales
- Food Service Sales
- Catering Sales
- General Retail Sales
- Fundraising
- Selling your art/design you created
- Anything else you can imagine
- "There's a market in everything" - Mark J. Perry

STEML ONLY

Based on knowledge, innovation, and research. Generally someone who is taught a skill in an academic setting. Operates on the concept of demonstration and repetition to disseminate ideas from one group to another. Constant testing of knowledge and demonstration of understanding through various challenges such as exams, papers, projects, dissertations, and state & federal licensing, etc. *Usually works as a part of a larger organization.* Examples:

- Professors
- Teachers
- Lawyers
- Marine Biologists
- Chemical Engineer
- Electrical Engineers
- Engineers in general
- Doctors
- Surgeons
- Nurses

Livelihood's Four Quadrants (2 of 2)

PADS + STEML

"Deadly combination." The highest probability of success. This involves selling your services as a STEML skill. *Usually works individually or starts their own small organization, which sometimes grows over time into a large organization.* Examples:

- Former electrical engineer at a major corporation retires and starts building and selling gadgets out of his/her garage or home office.
- Medical doctor who used to work at a hospital now runs his/her own family practice/clinic. The doctor needs to "sell" his/her services.
- Dentist at his/her dental practice needs to drum up new patients/clients. No patients means no cleanings, means no insurance reimbursements, means no money, means no livelihood.
- Lawyer sets-up his/her own law firm/practice and needs to sign-up clients to sell their services.

NONE OF THE ABOVE

These are the one-offs. Someone with no ability to *"sell"* and unable to learn or grasp STEML skills. Or someone who has no need to *"sell"* or learn skills to make a livelihood. Examples:

- Someone who inherited wealth. No need to make a livelihood as they live off the earnings of their wealth. Could be involved with philanthropy.
- Someone with no skills who is a factory laborer, custodian, general laborer, etc., doing repetitive tasks.
- Someone with moderately developed skills who is *"stuck"* in the service industry: assistants, clerks, etc.
- Someone with or without skills who joins any branch or part of the military or law enforcement.
- The public sector is a parallel universe. People can *also* make livelihoods with sales and STEML skills in government or non-profits.

The Four-Quadrant Framework

Quadrant 1. PADS Only

- Persuasion, art, design, and sales

- Referred to as *"soft skills"* or *"people skills"*

- Needs to convince someone else to exchange their resources *(often financial)* for the good or service

- Extends into various fields beyond traditional retail, such as entertainment and management

Quadrant 2. STEML Only

- Science, technology, engineering, math, and law

- Referred to as *"hard skills"* or *"hard sciences"*

- Exchanges and/or applies knowledge with others seeking to learn about a particular subject or to solve/complete a project

- Livelihood often follows a sometimes hierarchical path or structure within a larger organization

Quadrant 3. PADS + STEML

- *"Deadly combination,"* with the highest probability of success

- Beyond regular PADS—someone selling a *"hard science"* or a product/service based on STEML

- STEML, by its nature, has a captive audience due to the limited expertise, participation, and significant demand by large organizations and the public sector, so using PADS to benefit from STEML makes for a successful livelihood

Quadrant 4. None of the Above

- Someone who does not possess any PADS or STEML skills and is unable to learn them, must perform general labor, pure exchange of time for financial resources

- Someone who has plenty of financial resources and does not need to make a livelihood and instead can directly pursue his or her passions and goals

Let's explain each part of the framework with a few examples. In the following examples, we'll describe a typical livelihood of someone in each quadrant, regardless of their place on the Tri-Skills Framework. Recall that someone can fall into any of the quadrants and be in any of the three: alignment, misalignment, or borderline, as discussed in the previous chapter.

The following image shows this relationship between the Tri-Skills Framework and the Four Quadrants.

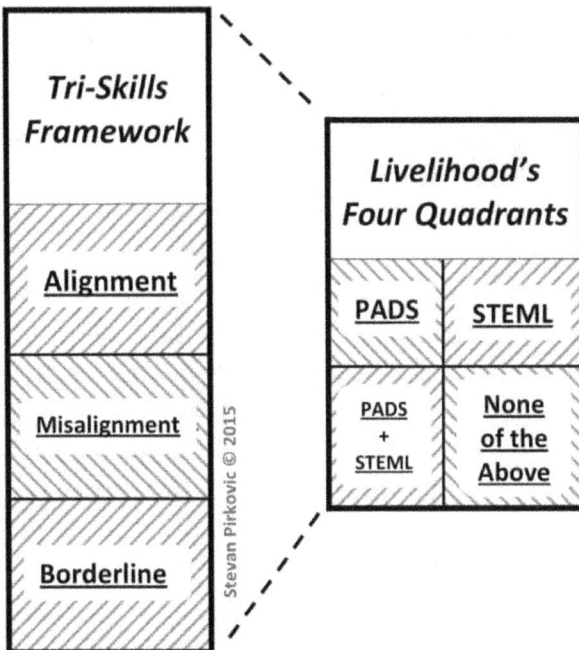

Let's take someone in the fields of art and design, for example. Granted that art and design are serious subject matters, they are not as stringent as the **"hard skills"** of STEML. Art and design develop more naturally in people compared to STEML skills. It's not as if a child grows up with the natural ability to be a chemist. You don't often hear someone say a child had a natural ability to mix together elements of the periodic table. They might have an interest in chemistry, and after some studying and training, they can acquire the skills of a chemist, but it's different compared to a child who is born with an artistic gift, like drawing or painting.

The story that you often hear is similar to what I just mentioned, in that a child might be a natural painter or skilled at drawing. PADS skills, such as painting, are more inherent in nature compared to STEML skills, which are more often learned and studied later in life. Because of this human inheritability of skills, such as art and design, they often require and are accompanied by correlated talents, such as persuasion and selling, hence PADS. Because what good would your skills be if you can't figure out a way to benefit from them or earn a living from them? (borderline)

Graphic artists, graphic designers, architects, interior designers, and professional painters, all need work from their clients. How many times will a graphic designer need to create a project for themselves? Probably a few times when they're working on a personal project, but for the most part, they need to convince clients and customers that their design is better than anyone else's. That's why customers are seeking the services of a graphic designer in the first place—they don't know the ins and outs of designing, or they'd do it themselves. That's why in a sea of graphic designers, a successful designer needs to be able to **"sell"** and convince clients that he or she is the best for the project.

# # #

The same goes for all the other PADS fields. Consider the idea that there now exists an entire field of project management and administration. CEOs, managers, and partners all need and want to *"sell"* everyone on their plan or vision for a particular organization. Their audience is often comprised of key stakeholders, such as investors, employees, and community members. No matter what they're selling, they will use all the tactics of PADS skills to achieve their goal or strategy.

Although the PADS skills are referred as the *"soft skills,"* they have gained a considerable amount of legitimacy throughout the years. Similar to the *"hard sciences"* found within the STEML skills, PADS has spawned fields such as consulting, management, organizational behavior, business intelligence, and project management.

#

Self-proclaimed America's Master Handyman Glenn Haege, says, *"Proper Prior Planning Prevents Poor Project Performance."* Concepts such as project manager professional (PMP), Six Sigma, Lean, and Green Belt, didn't exist 40 years ago, but have arisen from a combination and a mixing of PADS and STEML. Large-scale and small-scale projects in every sector of the economy utilize these PADS-oriented concepts to facilitate their success.

Unlike STEML fields, such as engineering and science, PADS credentials or qualifications, such as a master's degree in business administration (MBA) and Six Sigma, are practically inconsequential compared to their STEML counterparts. In my opinion, it is like trying to put a stamp of approval on a puddle of water, it just doesn't stick.

Trying to build and legitimize PADS is important, but the emphasis placed on these hollow academic-like structures is misplaced. If someone needs these credentials to help them *"sell,"* then they should pursue them. But an MBA or a PMP is not necessary for everyone in the PADS field, as people can be successful without them. The same is true for top executives in the C-suite.

Many believe that occupants of the C-suite (CEO, COO, CFO, and others) need these advanced credentials. But an overview of corporate America shows that for every one credentialed executive there is at least another who worked their way up through the ranks, either without credentials, or they earned them on their way up.

The value of these credentials, just like traditional STEML credentials, lies in the brand behind them. Training and education in both PADS and STEML will ultimately earn someone a successful livelihood, if they make the most of it. In the end, it's what you make of it and what you do with the credentials you've earned in that traditional four years at school, or the now more common five years.

A bachelor's or master's degree of art or science gives the bearer the tools, models, and mental frameworks to use to approach and tackle situations in a specific field of study. On the margin, the value of earning any of these credentials lies in the brand behind it. If you are driven and know your skills and passions early on, earning a degree in your field is just like mastering your skill and solidifying it. For these individuals, it doesn't matter which institution they attend, as they will be successful anywhere they go. But for the individuals who use their time in higher education to find their skill, brand matters.

On the margin, not just any bachelor's or master's degree will work. If you are just coasting along and floating through college with no rhyme or reason, the brand behind your institution will be the thing *"selling"* whatever impassionate skill you've learned along the way. The institution you attend to receive your training or education makes a difference. Like anything else, a brand name sells you, and it adds value.

Faculty references, alumni networks, studying environment, and name recognition all make a difference. If you've used your time in higher education to find your skill, you are going to need to rely on your credentials to help you find ways to make your livelihood. This is more true for the individuals who had to learn a skill compared to individuals who were mastering and enhancing their skill and can point to their past experiences and successes to use as their credentials.

#

A major theme behind finding your livelihood, and a simple theme at that, is, **"don't do it for the money."** Well, initially anyway. Simply trying to make yourself **"fit into"** a skill, or forcing a skill on yourself, does not always yield the best outcomes. Doing it for the money can lead you down a twisted and shady road. Billionaire steel maker (in today's money) Andrew Carnegie wrote in his book, **The Gospel of Wealth,** that idolizing money is dangerous. And as I mentioned earlier, this notion is echoed by others, such as futurist and author Alan Watts, and world-renowned author Nassim Taleb, who have been quoted as saying that one of the most addicting things in life, right up there with drugs and alcohol, is a salary or paycheck.

Blindly pursuing a livelihood just for the financial gain only enables you to just keep doing that particular job, only to keep on getting enough money to keep on doing that job. You'll never align your skills with your passions and goals by doing this.

If you specialize in a skill, and you become an expert in your field, success will follow. In one way or another, you'll be able to provide for yourself. If you can align your passions and goals, you'll be able to make a livelihood out of your skill.

Just remember to do your skill and do it well. Be the best at your skill, and the money will eventually follow. This harkens back to the economic theory we touched on in chapter 2: specialization. Recall that on a basic level, everyone has their own specialty and uses their skill to trade with others who have skills in other fields that they aren't well versed in to maximize efficiency. Take for instance, the classic country example.

Each country specializes in certain outputs, and they trade these outputs. Not to say that certain outputs are restricted to certain countries, it's just that some countries have certain outputs that are higher quality than others. Other countries are willing to trade their own prized outputs for something of higher quality from another country, because they don't possess the necessary skills or natural resources to produce that particular output.

So if you don't have a traditional skill from any of the STEML fields, then get into the universal skill of selling and persuasion. Try your hand at selling the work from someone else's skill. Get good at convincing others that your mousetrap is the best. Be the best seller and the money will follow.

In either case, you need to hone and perfect your skill. Even if you fall into the **"none of the above"** quadrant, just be the best you can be at your job. But if you are just picking your skill because you believe it's profitable, then a disconnect will occur. And it's been said before, like the often misattributed, yet still famous, Abraham Lincoln quote, "Whatever you are, try to be a good one."

In an ideal situation, you would have matched your skill to your livelihood and your passion. If there is a disconnect, then you will be working for something you don't believe in or don't even want to do, just to save up resources to do what you actually want to do, outside your work.

#

Within the context of the **Four Quadrants,** there is no **"right"** or **"wrong"** path to successfully make a livelihood. The only area where someone could get into trouble is if they can't find their skill in either PADS or STEML or a combination of both, and they can't learn a skill in the meantime to make a livelihood while they're finding their skill. This is a dangerous spot because it could potentially, and often does, create a situation where someone is disconnected from their passions and goals, because they don't possess the skills necessary to achieve them. Then they are stuck performing labor in the hope of one day being able to live out all, or at least part, of their passions and goals.

# # #

Questions that arise out of the idea of the *Four Quadrants* are:
   1. Is STEML only successful with PADS?

   2. Is PADS viable without STEML?

   3. Does PADS drive STEML, or does STEML drive PADS?

   4. Can success be achieved in none of the above?

Regarding questions 1 and 2, each skill set is naturally independent of the other. Each can be successful in providing a meaningful livelihood for anyone who possesses them naturally or learns them. It is not necessary to have both skill sets to be successful, but your chances of successfully making a livelihood increase dramatically if you possess both skill sets or at least have one and incorporate or utilize other people with the opposite skill set.

Livelihoods with STEML can certainly be successful without PADS, and vice versa. In terms of a larger picture, although both are independent, they really do need each other in the long term. The ideas, goods, services, and concepts that the PADS fields often ***"sell"*** came from, either directly or indirectly, or were inspired by STEML fields. Science and technology are responsible for many of the innovations and breakthroughs that create the products and services we use every day. Without the expertise of the PADS fields, many of these innovations would never see the light of day. This dovetails into question 3.

# # #

Regarding question 3, **Does PADS drive STEML, or does STEML drive PADS?** on some levels both PADS and STEML drive each other. PADS often demands new innovations from STEML, and STEML might also push new innovations onto PADS. There are varying degrees of pushing and pulling throughout time. Moreover, at any one point in time, the degree of influence of either PADS or STEML will vary from industry to industry and sector to sector.

Take the Bill Gates and Steve Balmer story, for example. Regardless of the origins of his first computer software MS-DOS, Bill Gates had some technical knowledge in computer programming and software. To the extent that he built Microsoft in the early days, Bill was definitely STEML oriented. But at the same time, he had to sell his software, which eventually made him a **"deadly combination."**

While his PADS skills might have been lackluster, he and Paul Alan managed to get sales going in the first years of Microsoft. When they realized they needed help in their efforts, they brought on the most extreme salesperson they could think of: Steve Balmer. Without question, Steve is PADS oriented. Did he have knowledge of software and computing? Yes. But he was first an MBA and a salesperson, and his selling brought him success, not the fact that he created software or related technologies.

Bill Gates is someone who was mostly STEML-oriented with some PADS skills. But when he required reinforcement in expanding his technology company, he needed help with PADs and hired Steve Balmer to boost his company and to sell the STEML that he created.

# # #

Regarding question 4, ***Can success be achieved in none of the above?*** someone who has no need for a skill, or who doesn't need a skill to achieve their goals or passions, could be considered successful by some definitions. But the entire idea of this framework is to find alignment between your skills, natural or learned, and your passions and goals.

Ultimately, people in this quadrant need to evaluate their own levels of success. Would you be happy if you had a skill, but you didn't need to use it to achieve your passions or goals? Would you be happy if you didn't have a skill, but knew you didn't need one because you were financially secure to pursue your passions and goals?

Everyone's answers to those questions will vary. And it ultimately comes down to your views about affluence and fortune. But the entire concept of this framework is for the majority of us who don't start off or spontaneously fall into this quadrant, at least not right away.

For argument's sake, let's assume that someone goes through life never finding their skill or is unable to learn a skill. They have a passion for fishing and love to fish recreationally. They are a factory worker, for example. They don't necessarily ***"love"*** working in a factory, but they can bear it because it's better than starving and doing nothing. They might even lie to themselves and say they ***"like it"*** and that it makes a decent livelihood. They punch in and out, day after day, working toward their annual vacation in Florida, and eventually their ultimate vacation, retirement.

In this scenario, the individual can be successful. Working and saving financial resources throughout the course of their lives in order to one day fully live out and pursue their passion of fishing, instead of once a year during vacation. Although their livelihood was totally misaligned, they managed to work toward their passion.

It would have been an easier and probably more bearable journey if they had found their skill and at least attempted to see how they could make a livelihood with it. But what if we looked at this same scenario and assumed that this person had no skills, worked in factory to make a livelihood, and had no passions or goals? This scenario is just downright depressing. Working day in and day out toward what? To retire someday? Retire to what? A life of what?

That's why it's important to ask yourself these questions as early as possible when you're trying to make your livelihood, as I mentioned in Chapter 3. This is easier said than done, and it's a difficult look inside yourself that might take months or even years, but it's worth it when you know what you can do and what you want to do.

# # #

Much of what I've covered can be seen portrayed in the life stories of others, as we'll see in the coming chapters. More interesting, it's also found in art; as I've discussed making a livelihood is an art. But you can call it a case of art imitating life, or life imitating art. As a universal art, I believe music is a great expression of human emotions, trials, tribulations, and amazing stories.

A great example is the aptly titled 2010 album, *You Get What You Give,* from the world-famous Zac Brown Band, showing that finding your skills, goals, and passions takes work. Some people are fortunate enough to find theirs early, like I mentioned, and others need to take their time. But you'll never know if you don't put in the time to find out.

In the hit single, *"Keep Me in Mind,"* Zac Brown Band sings about trying to start a relationship. The story is about a young man who is trying to court a woman, but she is already committed to someone else. He says that if she ever gets lonely or if things don't work out, that he'll always be there for her. He then says this legendary line:

> *"Life's too easy to be so damn complicated."*
> —Zac Brown Band

The young man knows that she's with someone else, but he keeps praying that one day they'll be together. To him life is easy, he loves her, and they should be together—simple. But relationships and emotions make things complicated, and she's with someone else. He knows that he can't change true love and that he can't change who she loves. So, just like the title of the song, he tells her to keep him in mind, if she ever has no one else to love.

Making your livelihood is a simple model. Find your skill, discover your passions and goals, and figure out how to align them as close as possible. But we all know that the everyday tribulations get in the way of finding our skills and passions. Just like how relationships and emotions get in the way of the young man from the Zac Brown song, life often gets in the way of us finding our skills and passions.

But if we put in the time to find them, we can truly make a livelihood. Because if you align your skills and passions, then you're truly not working. You'd be living your life while making your livelihood, and that is what sweet success is all about. Making your bread and butter and actually getting a chance to taste that crunchy bacon.

In the next four chapters, I'll review the stories of Kevin Plank, the CEO of Under Armour; Jonathan Winters, legendary comedian; Frank Kern, professional marketer; and Tony Robbins, motivational speaker. While each of them is successful in their own right, they are all great examples of the STEML vs. PADS dichotomy and the Four Quadrants. Their stories illustrate that there is no one right way to find your livelihood and that there are multiple paths to success.

Let's take a look.

6

Kevin Plank

Speaker: Kevin Plank (Under Armour CEO)

Date: November 7, 2013

Name: "Grow This House"

              GE Capital 2013 National Middle Market Summit

              Kevin Plank interviewed by

              Tom Keene of Bloomberg Surveillance

● ● **Key Points** ● ●

By all accounts, Kevin Plank's story is as picture perfect as it gets. He grew up in the affluent suburbs of Baltimore, Maryland. There was no apparent struggle in his story. His mother was a former mayor his hometown and later director of the Office of Legislative and Intergovernmental Affairs at the US Department of State. His father was a real estate developer in Virginia.

Kevin focused his childhood on sports, particularly the game of football. After high school, most kids usually go to college or a career, but not Kevin. He was interested in football and continued his passion for the game at a college preparatory school, Fork Union Military Academy. Despite graduating from Fork Union with an impressive class, 13 of his classmates were ultimately drafted into the National Football League (NFL); Kevin only managed to become a walk-on at the University of Maryland in College Park.

Nonetheless, Kevin continued on his path of passion for football and athletics in general. The rest of his story is history. He went on to found the athletic apparel company, Under Armour, and grew it to what it has become today, one of the top five apparel companies in the world, a company with a market capitalization of more than $13 billion.

While Kevin's story and rise to fame are interesting, what's even more interesting are his style and his philosophy. Kevin has done countless interviews and has been the focus of many articles throughout his life. The best interview he's given to date, in my opinion, is when he was a featured guest at GE Capital's 2013 National Middle Market Summit, hosted at The Ohio State University in Columbus, Ohio.

Kevin's mantra is *"Why not us?"* This is an incredibly powerful mindset to have. His focus throughout his career was to *"make the world's greatest T-shirt for football players."* His immediate goal was not to compete with the large existing apparel companies; it was to just help people who played sports by making a great product. This notion has many implications in business and in personal life, in terms of finding your livelihood. It's about the idea of specializing and focusing on your talent.

As I discussed in Chapter 3 about the *Tri-Skills Framework,* Kevin started in the path of *alignment.* He grew up wanting to play professional football, even attending special schooling for football. This was clearly his passion. Had he been able to play professionally, his livelihood would have been aligned with his goals and passions.

Instead, Kevin's livelihood now is based on the success of the company he founded. You could argue that he is in **misalignment,** because he is not playing football, but that's not to say that his passions and goals could have changed since wanting to play football as a child. And I believe they quite obviously have. His passion is his company and working to continue its success.

Examining Kevin more closely, we find that he falls into the PADS category **(persuasion, arts, design, and sales).** Kevin graduated from the University of Maryland with bachelor's degree in business administration (BBA). This degree doesn't offer its recipient any real skills, other than being **"a jack of all trades, master of nothing."** With a BBA, you know a little bit about everything, but you're an expert at nothing, unless you take it upon yourself to go the extra mile and actually master a skill.

But Kevin had an extra card up his sleeve. He was an expert at something. He did, after all, attend Fork Union Military Academy for football training, was classmates with future NFL players, and played at the college level for the University of Maryland. So I think it's safe to say that Kevin knew quite a bit about football, even though he didn't graduate with a **"bachelor's degree in football."**

This clearly puts Kevin in the **"sales only (PADS)"** quadrant of the four quadrants, as discussed in Chapter 5. He was just selling a product that he created. He wasn't a lawyer, doctor, or engineer by training. In fact, he wasn't anything from the STEML **(science, technology, engineering, math, and law)** category.

You could argue that because Kevin learned about sewing and fabrics, that he actually also falls into the STEML category. This is true—although he didn't have any formal training in the apparel industry, he was self-taught. Another description of Kevin would be that he is PADS (sales) and STEML to some degree. But sewing T-shirts was not his skill, so I would argue against this. Kevin didn't create or invent a new sewing machine that makes his shirts better that anyone else's. He developed the idea of making compressed stretchy T-shirts.

Compression and stretchy materials were already around, being used for other applications. He just brought them onto the athletic field, so to speak. Had he actually created or invented a new material or machine to make T-shirts, then I could argue that he was a self-taught engineer to some extent, but only creating a product with existing materials and technology, he falls into the PADS (sales) category.

This is why Kevin is relentless in anything he does, always wanting to be the best, and always asking, *"Why not us?"* He is like Larry Ellison or Steve Jobs, but his skill is in the apparel world. Neither Steve nor Larry was an expert in their field, but both were damn good salesmen of their time.

Take a look at Kevin's interview with Tom Keene on the next page.

Kevin Plank
Courtesy: Google Free Images

● ● **Begin Interview** ● ●

Narrator: Please welcome Kevin Plank, chairman and CEO of Under Armour. Interviewed by Tom Keene, host of Bloomberg Surveillance.

Tom Keene: They wanted me to be in the video, but they looked at my body and said no [chuckles]. First of all, I've got to tell you that I hate Keith Sharon. I have tickets to game six tonight for my Boston Red Sox, first home game win, World Series since 1918, and I'm in Columbus, Ohio. Just great. Just for Jeff [referring to Jeff Immelt, CEO of GE] and Kevin. This has been great, this has been fun to grow up in a manufacturing community, a place of middle markets, and to see this reinvigorating year three as you move forward, I think is great. I'm going to get right to it; the clock is ticking back there. We'll talk growth this hour; we'll get to that in a minute.

They're talking about what they did. We just heard about four subgroups, some underperforming and some performing and the single sentence I heard, is that they just talk about what they're doing, it's an indigenous process. Day to day, what do you talk about at Under Armour?

Kevin Plank: You were very easy to me this morning on television, so thank you very much.

Tom Keene: It was a wet kiss interview, this isn't.

Kevin Plank: But you're hard, you're fast. So I'm bracing myself right now, but I appreciate that. First of all, thank you very much for being here and among so many entrepreneurs and innovators in the room as well. And Jeff, thank you for hosting.

So, this is an important topic, that you know I'm glad I get the opportunity to have a microphone to tell you my point of view, as I think about it, because, professor, I thought you did a wonderful job, and congrats to the information that's being collected. Because data is key, data is critical for us. It's the way that we run and manage our business. But at the same time, I also believe there is point where there can be too much data. And there is a point where you need action.

I have a slogan that I've used since really the company started, that I say, "We're always smart enough to be naive enough to not know what we could not accomplish." I'll say it again. "We were smart enough to be naive enough to not know what we could not accomplish." And that means, that idea of "Why not us?" That idea of when we started, when I speak to older, smarter, board-type people and tell them that I had this idea for this stretchy compression T-shirt—

Tom Keene: Guys like Jeff Immelt?

Kevin Plank: [laughs]. No, Jeff actually has learned enough in time, like all of us, that we don't know everything. And those are the best leaders. And where, why can't we take on this other company? But when I started it was saying Under Armour was going to compete, we're gonna go beat brand X, brand Y, brand Z, and not unlike coach Urban Meyer [football coach for Ohio State University] last night at dinner, he won't say the guy up north's name, we won't say the guy out west's name either. So you'll hear me refer to "them," "the bad guys," "Darth Vader," things like that, but we sort of, we keep it in context.

But why couldn't we compete with them? And when we started it wasn't saying, "I'm going to build this massive brand that will go head-to-head or toe-to-toe with the biggest companies on the planet," it was "I'm gonna make the world's greatest T-shirt for football players."

And very quickly it grew from football players to one of the football players also played baseball, and then another one told the other guys on the baseball team, told the people on the lacrosse team, and then one of the girlfriends of the guy that he's dating on the lacrosse team said, this isn't just good for baseball, and football, and lacrosse players, the girls liked it too.

And the company began to grow as this very organic process of, allowing the consumer to pull us to new markets. Versus us just simply relying on a strategy of "we're going X, Y, and Z" and what does your business plan say? It was "What are they going to give us" and we'll go where we get it.

Tom Keene: How many years in were you, before you went from word-of-mouth to almost being a small business? To actually executing day-to-day?

Kevin Plank: That moment, for me, was when I realized I set out to build the greatest T-shirt company in the world for football players. And it was that "aha" when I realized it was baseball players, and lacrosse players, and it was women, as much as it was men. And it was going, wait a second—this isn't just a great new product, you know, this is an entire category. This is an idea; this has the ability to be a brand. And it wasn't some clairvoyant idea that I had like, "I know what I'm going to build," it was, "more importantly, tomorrow is gonna be better than today." You know, the next product, version two is gonna be a heck-of-a-lot better than version one.

Tom Keene: Give us an example of an early defeat.

Kevin Plank: Our women's business is a great one. So call it roughly 2002, we were on our way to being—we finished five million dollars in 2001—so our growth was, our first five years in business, going from zero to five million dollars. The second five years growing from five- to three-hundred million dollars.

Tom Keene: This is revenue, not your compensation?

Kevin Plank: Correct [laughs]. Yes.

Tom Keene: I just want to be sure.

Kevin Plank: It's a little different. The next five years growing from three-hundred million to two-eighty-five million to crossing the billion-dollar milestone, that was 2010. So fifteen years to the first billion dollars, and where we are as a company, now in an accelerated growth program, you know fifteen years to the first billion in 2010, and in 2012 we were 1.8 billion, this year we'll be more than 2.3 billion.

Tom Keene: But you got off track. Tell me about the destroyed women's business you did.

Kevin Plank: So, go back to 1995. And you're thinking, some of the best decisions that we've made as a company were the ones that we didn't do. The decisions that we didn't screw up. Our women's business was one of them. So we were just making unisex products. We were making one style of product. And men would buy it, and, as we got into the women's market, the smaller sizes started selling more. So when we decided to make a women's product around 2001–2002, we were about a five-million dollar business, and we had orders to the tune of about eight-hundred-thousand dollars at cost, about 1.5 million dollars were orders for women. And our first approach to the women's business was pretty simple. It was eight guys sitting around a table.

Tom Keene: Smart.

Kevin Plank: All talking about what our wives and girlfriends would like. And so the philosophy was effectively summed up as—

Tom Keene: Dean Poon, throw a football at him [referring to Christine A. Poon, dean of business at OSU].

Kevin Plank: It was easy, we shrink it, and we pink it. It's pretty simple, right? When you look at it. How hard can this be? She'll love this stuff. So I remember we used the same manufacturer, the same designers, the same fabrics, the same everything. And by the end of the day, I remember it was June, middle of June, I'm in our warehouse, the women's product shows up from all the manufacturers, we're ready to ship it out. And we'd already had ads in magazines; we promoted it and everything else. And I'm looking at this $800,000 of cost, $1.5 million of wholesale product we're about to sell. And I'm looking and saying, the stitching isn't right, the sizing isn't right, the color isn't right, and saying we can't do this. And I'll never forget, remember this is 15 percent of our revenues, and I'm going, "The worst thing I can do is damage our brand to women and send this product out there."

Tom Keene: Yeah.

Kevin Plank: So we made the very difficult decision to torch it. So we literally burned $1 million dollars' worth of product.

Tom Keene: And everybody in this room has this challenge every day. I mean every quarter, making sausage is tough. How do you get through that?

Kevin Plank: We were a private company at the time. And we knew that we hadn't disappointed our customer yet. And we never wanted to do that. Because brands are, as everyone in here knows, brands are all about trust. And trust is built in drops, and it's lost in buckets. So by not sending that out there, we need a different approach. We burned the product, we came back, and I told our customers, and it was really hard phone calls. And our customers came back and we said, "We'll be back in a year."

And we went out, and we didn't just hire a woman to take it on. But we hired a great head of women's product, a great head of women's marketing, a great head of women's production, and a great head of women's sales. And we built the piece to truly be great. If you wanna be great, you can't just say it. It's the difference between talking-the-talk and walking-the-walk. And I'm very proud today, where we went public in 2005; our women's business was less than 15 percent of our company.

Tom Keene: Right.

Kevin Plank: And we made the declaration that women's would someday be larger than men's. We have this very sort of rough-and-tumble masculine brand. And people laughed at us. Today, we've added over two billion dollars in revenue since 2005, and women's is now nearly 30 percent of our business.

Tom Keene: Well, within this, "Grow This House," the great statistic for me is that the tight T-shirt company, you went from 60 percent tight T-shirt down to 14 percent tight T-shirt. Where is that in five years? You're making tight T-shirts in five years?

Kevin Plank: Oh, of course. I mean we're today, at one point when we started we were 100 percent of the market. But we realized that our access point in, and you look at different brands you know, one brand invented the soccer boot, another brand invented the running shoe. You know our entry into being an authentic brand was building this compression T-shirt. So we started in 1996, we're the only company in the world doing it. And then very quickly it's this balance between I want to be the only one doing it, but I need to validate my market. So frankly as competition came on, it was about expanding beyond just that one singular core product. And not making us vulnerable to if someone else knocks-off that same product, they can take us out.

Tom Keene: On a growth basis, that's my key question for this entire two hours, right? This is the key question. What is the process to move beyond the success? It's so easy to be successful, and that really disruptive moment is fear of success. You were successful, but you've gotta move on. Was it just saying, go get women's, go get kids, or was it a more nuanced process from that to get to the next growth level?

Kevin Plank: It's reinvention. It's guardrails of growth. You know I had a business plan that probably wouldn't have gotten a "B" in your school initially, Dean Poon. You know I look at where we worked, and we've been flexible. You know since our IPO road show in 2005, you know we said there are five key growth drivers—men's apparel, women's apparel, footwear, international, and direct to consumer. And here we are eight years later. And we still have effectively had those five same growth drivers.

What we've done is that it's changed very much inside of it. And we've allowed ourselves to be entrepreneurial. We've allowed the leaders to take ownership to control and empower my team where, you know the hardest thing anyone in the "middle" has, is that, I'll never forget somebody, the person that says, "You know I signed every check, I know everything that happens in my organization, I see everything that goes on."

And that pride, and my reaction, I sort of started business that way, and I'll never forget a really smart guy who looked at me one day and said, "You mean you can't find anybody else to sign checks?" And it was going, "You know what? If I do allow someone else to do that, I can spend more time on the product. I can spend more time on the story. I can spend more time talking to my customers and selling my vision of what I want my company to be versus the little things." So moving on, and allowing yourself to be confident enough to, I know what I'm good at and I'm gonna provide this shared vision and we're all gonna tackle it.

Tom Keene: Right, we're here with GE Capital. And I read this of Jeff—I'm gonna write the biography of Jeff Immelt—but it will go to five volumes, and I'm like waiting from ten years from now. He was mentored by a guy named Pat Bales, which was plastics in Detroit or someplace like that. And the whole thing was based on skepticism of the home office. How do you develop that healthy skepticism of your 7,000 employees? They're looking back at you going, "Hey big shot in Baltimore, yeah, maybe not." How do you listen to their skepticism?

Kevin Plank: I run every meeting the same way. And I hope it's something that translates; I believe it's something that translates through our company. This is what I heard. This is what I think. This is what we're gonna do. So when we have a conversation, we have a topic come up of vision, direction, and where are we going. I end the meeting the same way, and we do a round table, and everyone goes around and they say it, and I'll take notes and I'll come back and I'll say okay. Here is what I heard everybody in here say. Right. Now let me give you my opinion as to why I feel it and why I see it. And then I encourage a little more dialogue and debate. And then at the end of it I say okay.

And this is an old football truism, it is. It's basically—this is the huddle. And we all get around and we say okay. I've got everyone's opinion, everyone's input. And you know this is a democracy but it's a kind democracy, a bit more of a dictatorship. At some point, somebody has to make the decision. In here are the entrepreneurs, and the principles, and the presidents that have to make that call. But at the end of the day I say, this is what we're going to do. And they have to trust that I listened to them.

Because the constituents that are at my table are representative of the team that I have out in the audience. And that they have someone and they have a voice, and that the women's team has a voice, and that the global team has a voice, and that retail has a voice, and wholesale has a voice. And every one of those perspectives has to shape what ultimately my job is to make the call and say "I hear you, but I believe this is the direction we need to go."

Tom Keene: As middle market and 7,000 employees—how do you respond to the media cliché of talking about Mulally [referring to Ford's CEO Alan Mulally] and One Ford, and what they're trying to do out at Microsoft, that's another big company out on the west coast, like One Microsoft and that, is there a One Under Armour?

Kevin Plank: You know, I think we're struggling right now, where we find ourselves is that we've done a good job of establishing ourselves as a North American wholesale almost apparel company. And we still get plagued with that. Meanwhile we have a full suite of products from equipment to footwear, primarily.

Tom Keene: I'm watching Tottenham Hotspur every weekend, NBC sports [referring to soccer team in the English Premier League].

Kevin Plank: Yes, you're a Spurs fans?

Tom Keene: Spurs? I have to. I'm on stage with you, I have to be.

Kevin Plank: [laughs].

Tom Keene: What are you doing in English Premier League football, talking about international? You're not an American company anymore.

Kevin Plank: Investing—more than 90 percent of our business is still based here in the U.S. What I've found is that anywhere we grow, and the way that we find to grow new products, like going from apparel to making footwear. New distribution, being good a sporting goods, places like Dick's Sporting Goods and the Sports Authority, and saying now we need to be relevant at FootLocker and FinishLine in the malls. Or new geography's going from being successful in America, saying we're now going to be successful in China, we're gonna be successful in Europe. It takes time. It takes investment. I've used this seven-or eight-year rule

Tom Keene: What's that rule?

Kevin Plank: It's not going to happen right away. We have a partner in Japan. We started doing business there at the end of

1998, beginning of 1999. From 1999 to 2007, our partner in Japan grew from zero to thirty-five million US dollars. Like slugging it out—$2 million, $3 million, $7 million, eight years getting through this process. Then all the sudden something happened. The tipping point occurred. And from 2007 to 2008, they went from $35 million to $72 million, $72 million to $90 million. This year they'll be nearly a quarter billion dollars in sales.

Tom Keene: What was that "something happened" within the Japanese culture?

Kevin Plank: It was the trust. It doesn't happen right away.

Tom Keene: You call that field credibility?

Kevin Plank: Yes, for us, for a consumer to believe in our brand, lots of people can make stuff. Lots of people can make shoes and they can make shirts. But there is something about Under Armour. There's something about brand. You know, brand makes you believe. Brand makes you believe that without, it can do this, but with it, it can go here. Now I can march a dozen scientists in here and tell you why I can make the best product in the world, the best apparel, the best footwear, anything that bears the Under Armour mark is something that, first of all, starts from the point of view that it will give the athlete an advantage. That's the trust. But there's also another thing.

I told this story last night at dinner. But, you know, I've witnessed the power of what brand does. So brand is the following. I'm in a sporting goods store in the Pacific Northwest of all places. I'm watching a mother and two kids, eight years old and ten years old on each hand. About four-o'clock in the afternoon, right after school. And the mother and the kid are walking through, shopping. All of a sudden, the little eight year old just looks, and stops his mom, and goes, "Mom, Mom, look, Under Armour, Under Armour."

And the mom kinda gives that look like, "Oh don't go over there, that stuff is expensive, don't do it." And I'm watching this, and I'm kinda goin', "good, good."

The kid breaks away, Mom get distracted for a second. He grabs one of our shirts. He takes the shirt, he pulls it over his little head, squeezes it down like this. All the sudden he's got this little compression shirt on, and the collar is sorta jacked up on the underside. He looks at his mom, he yells, he goes, "Hey, Mom, look at me. I'm wearing Under Armour. I can do anything!" That's brand.

The question when you walk into an Under Armour store is not "How can we help you or what can we do for you today?" The question is "What do you want to be?" Because the little boy may have thought, "You know what, I was gonna go out for the team, but I don't know; those guys are really fast."

Tom Keene: Define the distinction. I talked to Eddie George today; he was a football player at this school a few years ago.

Kevin Plank: Yes [chuckles]. I'm familiar with him.

Tom Keene: Okay, you're familiar with him. I talked to Eddie George, and he was raving about your work.

Kevin Plank: Eddie and I went to prep school together, by the way. Fork Union Military Academy. Eddie and I both went there to learn, "character." Right, Eddie?

Tom Keene: What was the first day like?

Kevin Plank: Yeah, oh my god. It sucked so bad.

Tom Keene: Continue [laughs].

Kevin Plank: 17 years old, I guess 17, just turning 18 years old.

Tom Keene: And you knew everything.

Kevin Plank: I was brilliant. I mean literally, nobody could tell me a thing. And then you realize how much dumber you get every day, and you hope you get a little smarter. But we're at Fork Union—you're out there, doing your running test. Eddie will remember this, there were 125 people on our post-graduate team, and we ended up having; coach just started putting us through three-a-day football practices to get the numbers back. And Fork Union was a place where a lot of guys went there to develop, get a little older, mature a little bit. Some guys went there for grades. But we had this special class, which is actually one of the things that led to Under Armour, as much as anything else.

In our one prep school class, we had 23 guys from our prep school class sign division 1-A scholarships. Thirteen of those guys wound up getting drafted to the NFL, three of which ended up being first-round draft picks, including one Heisman Trophy winner, which was Eddie. And you look at that team.

So where did Under Armour come from? Was it, you know, again this really clear moment that I had about the product? Everything is product, don't get me wrong. But it was as much as being recognized in this network of people that I had at 22–23 years old. My friends from high school that were now playing in the NFL. My friends from Fork Union that were in the NFL. My friends from the University of Maryland now in the NFL. This collection of 40 or 50 guys, that I knew well enough to call on the phone and say, "I've got an idea. Let me send you a shirt. If you like it, wear it. If you really like it, give one to the guy in the locker room next to you."

Tom Keene: But I look out an airplane window and I see a GE engine and there's just something about that. That's a brand development over, you know, all the work of aviation and engineering and that. How do you link brand to celebrity? Eddie George is a celebrity. But at the same time, it's not about celebrity. I don't equate Under Armour with celebrity. I equate it with a brand. How do you play that game?

Kevin Plank: I think it's a very delicate balance to creating the impression that we're not paying the most. Which is why people participate with our brand. We'll pay market, we'll take care, and we'll be fair with the celebrity endorsers that we have, that utilize and that help us sell our product, to help us relate. But you can't rely on—it's so shortsighted.

And there's a trend that just happened in our industry in Asia, around the Beijing Olympics in 2008. There was a number of companies that came out. And so when we went to China, for instance, we were competing against three or four global brands that you've heard of. And then there were seven or eight brands that went public in China, right around 2008, all with market caps in excess of $2 billion dollars. And the model, the formula they took was; we see how easy this is.

These companies, they sign athletes, they put shoes on them, and they sell and market their shoes. Of the $20 billion dollars of market cap that used to exist with those eight companies, I think it's down close to three or four billion dollars of market cap now maybe. And at the end of it, there'll be one or two survivors that will come of it.

If our brand is simply relying on, "Buy this product because of a celebrity endorser," it needs to start long before we put the Under Armour logo on it. It needs to be the point of view and the consumer needs to take us, or we need to make a deliberate decision as to why we're going down any particular market that we try to tackle.

Tom Keene: How do you delegate—well, let me back up—How do you choose managers, and how do you delegate managers? You've got 7,000 people. That means you need to know 50 or 60 executives really well.

Kevin Plank: Yeah, that. You know, leaders will typically choose themselves. You know, leaders always have one thing in common—they always have a herd. So it's pretty easy. Everybody gets a six-month pass, maybe a one-year pass. But at the end of one year, you bring a new leader on; you elevate somebody and say, you're now in charge of this division, this team, this product. And at the end of the year it's not going, "Here's your sales, how is your revenue growth, how did you do?"

We're growing at lightning speed. The question I have for them is, "Tell me about your team" "Who did you hire, who did you attract?" Because people don't quit companies, they quit people. And that's one thing we've learned and that we struggle with, frankly as much as anything else, of how do you make sure that; I'm most worried about the 27 year old who interned at Under Armour, and now she works in our e-commerce group, she's been there for five years, she went to Chapel Hill, but she's got a girlfriend that works at LuluLemon or works at Google or Facebook. And she's hearing how things are there. Am I truly moving her up through the system?

Tom Keene: How do you do that? I mean, this is a huge problem. These kids are impatient.

Kevin Plank: They're incredibly impatient.

Tom Keene: I've got my staff with me. Two of them may quit before I get back to New York.

Kevin Plank: [laughs]. There's three things I care about from human resources. And this is what I've come to—recruiting, onboarding, and development—right? We need to recruit the best talent. We need to make sure that we are best in class and have second to none in the way that we can do to attract people. So we spent, building up our company, building up our city. You know, focusing on Baltimore and making our other outer offices a place that people want to come and be compelled to, you know.

The second is onboarding. Making sure that we have our arms open—that you know you're joining a family. You're not just joining someplace that just provides a paycheck.

And the third is development. It's telling people how they do. And we're not excellent at any one of these pieces yet. So what we do, because we don't have all the processes like a GE who is world class in their ability for human resource development. Where I just simply host lunches. I'll host two lunches a month with these up-and-comers in groups of eight to ten at a time.

And I make my VPs, the 37 VPs that we have in the company, that they have to have lunch with five of their up-and-comers every single month. And if nothing else, if we don't have the process that gets you there, it goes such a long way to just say, let me just touch you and say, great job, you're doing a phenomenal job.

Tom Keene: I got to, and I'll pull the plug in here for LinkedIn. And I know Jeff's writing for LinkedIn as well. This idea that, and I've said this three or four times recently, there's nothing like going to lunch or going to dinner to get away from the expected business conversation.

Kevin Plank: Right.

Tom Keene: There's just nothing like food.

Kevin Plank: I've always been one of the youngest guys in the room, you know, and so you get up and all the sudden you've got gray hair and you're starting to age—

Tom Keene: Really [sarcastically]?

Kevin Plank: And you realize you definitely feel it. I'm 41 years old. And I start to do, one of the things that I can put in place. You know I just had a trip through Asia, and, prior to leaving, you know, I grabbed two young up-and-comers, one from finance and one from strategy. And I said, "You know, we're all gonna get plane tickets and we're all going over together. And you put them in the room and for nothing more than just the context—

Tom Keene: Absolutely, totally agree.

Kevin Plank: Of how developing them, where it's not just me sitting here and saying "I get to sit with the president of this or the CEO of that." But I want them to have that experience, for nothing else, and you have to be clear, with some of these young ones, they're aggressive, particularly the sales guys they talk sooo much. And you have to tell them, the point of you being here is to sit there and feel the energy and watch it. If there's an awkward pause in the room, it's probably intentional like—

Tom Keene: How long is your meeting? How long is your typical meeting?

Kevin Plank: Like a Chinese negotiation in a Chinese room—like this awkward Chinese pause is something we've called it. You know where the chairs are usually, you know you sit on a chair and the chair is this big. And you're sitting across a room. You've got these vendors on the other side. You know, they'll wait out. And as Americans, especially me, I've got this, "I've gotta break this silence, I can't keep it anymore." But I've learned in my old age, hopefully gathering some wisdom, and sometimes just let it bake.

Tom Keene: In the time we've got left. We've got five minutes left. I wanna talk about this serious idea, and there's all the branding and the image and that. There's also the financials. You are responsible for the four accounting statements. Grow This house. That's a complex financial dynamics. How do you handle that? When you look at unit dynamics or price dynamics, the top of the income statement, as you come down the income statement, you go over to cash flow or over to EBITDA [earnings before interest, taxes, depreciation, and amortization] on the balance sheet, how do you measure to double your growth, given the really challenging goals you have?

Kevin Plank: In the eight years we've been public, we've averaged 31 percent top line growth and 31 percent bottom line growth. You know that equal balance between those two things. But I'll start by saying that Under Armour is a $10 billion dollar brand, currently doing $2 billion dollars in business. And the old me, in prior to being a public company, but I still believe in a lot of this, the top line solves not all problems, but it solves a lot of your problems. And so, as we continue to make a point of demonstrating leverage on the operating line, you know, it's 10bps [basis points] and 20bps, because we're still investing in our business. I'm still investing in Japan. I'm still investing in China and investing in Brazil. And it's critical that we continue to do that.

But what we tell our shareholders, number one, we'll demonstrate leverage on the operating line, but I'm also a dollar invested with us, on a longer-term growth projection of 20–25 percent, and we've done 14 quarters in a row of 20 percent plus of top-line growth. A dollar invested in us, no matter what, it's going to be worth 20–25 percent more a year from now.

And we can't control the markets, and we can't control the way our investors view that. But we know the model that we have. And luckily, because we have these five balanced growth drivers. It's coming from a lot of different places. So I don't have to say, by any measure necessary you know, we've got to grow women's, so I've gotta ship that product that maybe didn't meet the measure that we have for our brand. And that's the balance.

Look, I'm gonna take a financial question, and I'm gonna cleverly turn it into a brand question. You know, I believe brands are like stories. You know, every story has a beginning, middle, and an end. And every product that we build, every athlete we sign, and every place we show up, from a distribution standpoint, is like a chapter in the book of our story. And chapter one needs to make sense to chapter two to chapter three to chapter four. So when I got all along back in 2002, and people would say things to me like "You guys need to make shoes." And I'd say, "I know we need to make shoes, we're just not there yet."

And so this natural progression that we have of whether it's being global, or whether it's getting into footwear. We're not launching new categories; we're trying to become excellent in the market where we're currently doing business and the categories we're currently doing business in.

Tom Keene: I wanna talk a little bit about education. You're committed to your University of Maryland. You're the uniforms? I mean please, what do they cost?

Kevin Plank: This isn't an education question [laughing].

Tom Keene: What do they cost? I mean come on. Nobody is on Twitter, there's no prosecutors.

Kevin Plank: I mean Maryland is entering the Big 10 next year, and so I took the time this morning, between sitting with you and driving around campus, and getting a sense of what the Big 10 was gonna look like. So it's absolutely intimidating. But apparently, I don't think we've spent enough on what the uniforms are gonna need to cost to dress out against Ohio State next year.

Tom Keene: Design some uniforms for the New York Giants; they need it.

Kevin Plank: Yes [chuckles].

Tom Keene: And final thought here on education. You're here at the Fisher College of Business, Ohio State University. You're in front of those kids, big success, and ancient at 41 years old. What is your advice to them about what **not** to do, everybody has got the "to do," but what's your advice about what **not** to do?

Kevin Plank: Don't read your own headlines. You know, and again, there's a lot of great data, there's a lot of great information that comes over, and I'm not saying don't read the newspaper. I want people to know, be informed. You know, understand what's happening out there, but don't allow that to limit you. Don't allow the pundits on the talking-head shows, apologies, but don't allow them to talk you out of it [referring to Tom Keene as a host of a TV show].

We started, I started, a T-shirt company in 1996. And I remember one of the first offices that we tried getting into on the inner harbor of Baltimore. We were rejected, because we were not a technology company. And they wouldn't allow us to go in there, and I'm thinking to myself, like God how can you call us not a technology company. Which had me saying, we should probably be a technology company too.

And the Under Armour of the future is not going to be this company that makes sweatshirts and sneakers. You know, we'll continue to make those products, but they'll be the most innovative and technologically beneficial products in the world. And the way that we'll approach that, will be through a whole host of proactive things that we'll do. You know, I caution people when they say, "Are you gonna invest that? You hear what people are saying. We're in the middle markets. Middle means $10 million to a billion. The odds of where we all feel the sort of strain of the economy and the larger broader issues that are happening out there.

But I, you know, I coined a term in 2007 for my company that I called, "No Loser Talk." And no loser talk means that people weren't allowed to say things like, you know in spite of what's going on out there, we were able to achieve 11 percent growth, or 14 percent this, or 14 percent that. Get over it. Like there is a reason. There are companies that are growing. There are companies that can move. And you don't need a list of reasons as to why something didn't happen versus finding one really good one as to why it can happen.

Tom Keene: We're outta time. We're in overtime here right now. Quickly, a louder, more focused, more disruptive voice. The word disruptive is so in right now. Clay Christenson gets like 10 cents every time somebody says disruptive. A disruptive voice, where are you gonna be in five with your disruptive voice?

Kevin Plank: We'll meet all of our financial goals, number one. But number two, we will be away from solving problems that athletes have had, to solving problems that athletes will have. Proactive medicine is the next generation for us. Of not allowing people to rely on a doctor's visit every 12 or 24 months and something hidden in a manila envelope that tells you what your health is. Your health should be a proactive measurement. A piece of data that's updating you on a daily basis, that allows you to track yourself of where you've been, where you are, and most importantly where you're going.

Tom Keene: Kevin Plank, thank you so much.

Kevin Plank: Awesome, thank you, thank you very much.

●　　●　　**End Interview**　　●　　●

7

Jonathan Winters

Speaker: Jonathan Winters
(comedian and improvisation artist)

Date: December 4, 2007

Name: Jonathan Winters—EG Conference

Getty Center in Los Angeles, California

Jonathan Winters Self-Directed Interview

● ● **Key Points** ● ●

Comedic genius doesn't even begin to describe Jonathan Winters. Winner of two Grammy awards for best comedy albums and nominated several times during his career, Winters was always at the forefront of comedic improvisation for nearly four decades. Winters doesn't mince words when he says at one point in his life, after returning from the Marine Corps, that he didn't know what he was going to do with his life. He bounced around a few jobs before he found his passion in art.

But Winters didn't have any solid skills he could use to make a livelihood outside of his passion for art. He tried several different jobs, such as working at a Coca-Cola bottling plant and doing the weather reporting for a radio station. But none of his jobs were bringing home the bacon for him and certainly not supporting his passion for art. Winters' passion for art wasn't producing a livelihood for him or his family. His livelihood was misaligned. He was working various jobs to gain resources to pursue his passion for art. But later on, Winters discovered his skill—the gift of gab. He was a natural comedian and improvisation actor. He had this skill all along, but never knew it.

While Winters' comedic routine and stand-up are hilarious, what's more interesting is his story and how he found his way into his livelihood. It took Winters nearly his entire young adult life to find his skill for comedy and improvisation. Winters has told his story through countless interviews at different points in his career. But I think the best interview he gave was when he was invited to speak at the EG Conference in 2007 at the world-famous Getty Center in Los Angeles, California. While having been out of the entertainment limelight at that point, Winters speech at the Getty provided a wonderful retrospective on his career.

Winters mentions that he was a unique child growing up. But he had always dismissed his persona and antics, never thinking he could turn them into anything. But it was his natural talent that was right in front of him his whole life that would be the key to him finding his livelihood. Eventually Winters found his way into show business.

After transitioning from a local radio station in Dayton, Ohio, to working at a local television station in Columbus, Ohio, Winters asked his boss for a $5 raise, after two-and-a-half years on the job. It was his employer's refusal to award Winters a raise that set the wheels in motion for him to take a risk and try to strike it rich in New York City. Winters was already married with a young child at the time he started to make in-roads in show business in New York. And it was comedy, in particular, where Winters developed his skills for improvisation. Winters' skills and passions had become aligned more or less compared to most people, once he found his skill.

Similar to Kevin Plank, Winters' comedic skills are PADS-based. He could create and spin webs of relatable and funny stories on a whim. And he did so, amazingly, throughout his career. But just like anyone else in the PADS fields, especially entertainment, he had to work hard at differentiating himself from other comedians and actors.

And this is why Winters' story is so powerful. He could have lived on working odd jobs to support his family and continued to pursue his passion for art when time allowed. But at some point, he discovered what he already had inside him, his skill for comedy and improvisation.

He used his skills to make a meaningful livelihood for himself and his family. And luckily, for Winters, he was able to align his passion for art more closely with his skill for comedy, compared to before he discovered his skill when he was just doing a job he didn't like that didn't use any of his skills.

Let's take a look at Jonathan's speech.

Jonathan Winters
Courtesy: Google Free Images

●   ●   **Begin Speech**   ●   ●

Please remain standing [walking out onto the stage]. Well, we made it down. Hit a couple of people coming down, but they were old anyway. There's always somebody that believes that.

"He struck two people and telling us about it."

Better to tell you about, than read it in the paper. Well, I guess I'll sit down, or either fall down. People say to me, and they say to all of us,

"How do you feel? How are you?"

I'm down to this, "O.L.D." It doesn't stand for Oldsmobile. I'm telling you, gang—don't get old. You begin to look old, the body, hey, the mind, eh, oh, abandoned. The rest of it is just like hot lava. You see old people working out,

"One, two, three, four" [referring to someone lifting weights].

Stuff hangs its terrible. Well, they said you know you could talk about anything you wanna talk about. I guess you might want to know how I got into this crazy business. I'm still wondering.

Mother and Dad were divorced when I was seven. We're not gonna get into heavy things, because there are families here.

"Oh, God, he's not gonna talk about Mother and Dad!"

I'm not, ha. But they got divorced, they were mad at each other. And they'd come in and look at me; I guess I was a problem. And it was always,

"What is he doing? What is he doing?"

I wasn't doing anything, I was just sitting there. There were no toys; they sold them. I was an unusual child, and I'm an unusual old man. And they were not the greatest audience. It was always,

"What is it? What do you want?"

They were always annoyed,

"What do you want? What do you want?"

How about a hug?

"Are you gay?"

No, just different [flings his hand through his hair].

At any rate, I just couldn't win. Any rate, I was an only child, and I knew somehow, that from seven and on, that I'd have to entertain myself. I didn't, you know, I wasn't getting the kind of affection that I thought I was gonna get. I'd watched Robert Young and Lee Remick too long. And the little white fence and the hugging and kissing [referring to the picture-perfect life depicted in the 1960s television show].

I went to the movies a lot. My dad took me to the movies. He told me he was a salesman, and he'd drop me off at about ten o'clock in the morning. This is back in Dayton, Ohio, where I grew up— well, my first seven years. And I had an uncle, I guess his cousin, he was an uncle to me—Uncle Billy who had the Realto Theater. So my old man would drop me off about ten o'clock in the morning and Uncle Billy who owned the theater, he was a projectionist. And I got to really know Hopalong Cassidy. You have about nine hours of Hoppy, you know, and you're wondering out the place,

"Hey, hey here you go" [making the shape of a gun with his hand].

I was sticking people up when I was nine.

"Arr, I'm Hoppy's son" [referring to a 1950s western movie].

Any rate, and later on in life, as I'm still a Hoppy fan. He's long gone now, but Hopalong Cassidy—my wife and I were in Paris, once in our lives, in 1957, and we were staying at the Plaza Athenee, and we went up four or five floors, opened the cage, and there was Hoppy [referring to the actor William Boyd]. And I, I'm like a lot of us, you know, I wanted an autograph—if you're an autograph person, you wanted to get an autograph. I was just stopped in my tracks. I just thought, God; I turned to my wife,

"Aileen, this is Hopalong Cassidy, William Boyd, okay?"

"Okay."

"What do you mean okay?"

"How about having a drink, Hop?"

Well, he was just like he was in the movies. He was even better; he was just the most down-to-earth guy. It was such a great thrill to go down to the bottom of the hotel, down to the lobby and into the bar and have a couple of drinks with him. Great guy.

I never really thought I was going to get into the business. My mother was in radio in Springfield, Ohio. She had women's programs, somewhat like Barbara Walters, kind of where she interviewed people. Because you don't get too many celebrities coming through Springfield. Lot of farm people, you know.

"I'll talk about my cows; I got some oil stains, mmkay!"

Umm, she had Arlene Francis on one time, and it was just before I went into the Marines. I guess I was about 15; I was 17 when I went. And, of course, 15, I went in, and I sat in the studio and my mother was to interview Arlene Francis, who was doing a play in Columbus, Ohio. And if you were doing a play, or you had written a book, or anything like that, you went all around these smaller cities to plug your book or your play. I remember Miss Francis turned to my mother and said,

"Are you to interview me?"

And my mother said,

"Yes, I'm Alice Balman."

It was her stepfather's name, you see.

"And I'll be interviewing you."

And Miss Francis turned and said, it was the first time I'd heard this,

"This is kind of a Mickey Mouse station."

And my mother said,

"Yes, and you're our Mickey Mouse guest."

So, you didn't step on my mom, man. Boy she'd come right back. But I had heard, she did a lot of plays and did twenty-five, thirty years of radio. I went in the [Marine] Corps. I just had to get away—period. I was terrible, and I know there are a lot of people out here that are scientists and math people who love math. I guess my label has been a combination of bipolar and manic-depressive. I've chosen polar, because we've been around the cape.

So at any rate, first grade, my dad would say to me, if he was sober,

"If I give you four apples and three more, how many do you have?"

If I had seen the apples, that could have helped me. But they weren't there, and I thought I had a pretty good imagination but,

"Four apples and three more, c'mon, c'mon."

And I said,

"Too many for the lunch box."

And he shook me, and he said,

"You're the dumbest white kid I know."

Good fun thing to tell me, and I got as far as plane geometry, and it was over. And the teacher, Mr. Sanders, turned to me and said,

"Your old man was right. You're the dumbest kid I ever taught."

And I said "Mr. Sanders"—never talk back to an older person by the way—I said

"Mr. Sanders, one thing about a dummy, he's strong. This is empty [points to his head], *but the body works. I could pick your ass up and throw you through the window."*

That was the only time I used that word in front of a mathematical person. And from there I went to the Marines. And I spent almost three years, finally made corporal. And I constantly heard,

"Is that the best you could get?"

No, the best I could get is to survive. I went up in the attic, I'll never forget, I collected toys, I still collect toys today, from the [19]30s and the [19]40s, and they're a lot more expensive today than when I was a kid. Toys then, little iron toys, some tin toys made in Japan, Germany, France, England, and here in America, were a dollar apiece, because we had come out of the Depression.

So I had a little trunk full of stuff, a fishing reel, a Shakespeare reel, had a 20-gauge shotgun, I had hoped to use on some people ha, ha, but we won't single them out, at any rate, and my ball glove, and baseball. I went to my mother and said,

"What happened to my toys? My toys are gone"

And she said,

"Well, we gave them to the mission."

Okay, you should have notified me, because I would have liked, there are some things I wanted to salvage. And my mother said,

"Well, how did we know you're gonna live?"

Well, you see, you can forget the hug. At any rate, I didn't know what I was gonna do. I knew I had to get to work because my mother said,

"You're gonna have to work. You're not just gonna lay around here. You're gonna have to pay rent, $25 a week. "

For rent, I thought that was a little high, you know. Especially where I slept, which was in a tree, nah, but actually, I was in the house, to clarify that.

At any rate, I worked at several kinds of jobs. Coca-Cola, I'll always remember Coca-Cola. I put in, I was in the washing—everything was a dollar an hour at that time in the [19]40s. It seemed to me, well, all the jobs I took were a dollar an hour. But of course my intelligence didn't carry me to two dollars.

So I'd take these six bottles of Coca-Cola, and go in the washer. You'd just pick 'em up like that [makes a hand motion] and wash them. And the guy came to me one day, and he said,

"Winters, how would you like to be an inspector?"

Well, I remember in the service, you know, ha, ha, being singled out.

"How would you like to go up there? Ha, ha" [points to the distance, referring to an objectionable location].

But somehow the dummy once again, you know. Okay, you get a stool, and you sit on a stool. Boy that brand new white shirt with the red stripes, and a big green Coca-Cola thing over here [points to shirt pocket]. And there was a fluorescent lamp and this track of Cokes going through [makes a passing hand motion]. Coca-Colas and you just looked for dead mice and marbles. I had an early condition of palsy when I was in my early twenties. So, at any rate, I gave that up, went to a few other jobs.

And then I went to college for about an hour. And I failed—of all things, I was always good in history—American history. They had medieval history, and I failed it by 3/16th of a grade, and I thought Charlemagne was a drink. So I was asked to, you know—I left before they told me I had to go. I said I was going downtown, and I never came back.

Then I decided I wanted to be an artist. And my dad said, he was all, and my mother said,

"Oh my God . . . an artist" [sobbing].

They whined you know. I said,

"Don't worry about it, the government will pay for it."

They said,

"Ohhh."

It was then that I met my wife. She's here today, and my son, my daughter came down to stare at Daddy, you know.

"Be articulate, don't wander" [makes blank face and darts eyes about].

But I tell ya' as I sit here in this chair—I guess they made in therapy—that had it not been for my wife, I wouldn't be sitting here or any place today. I was in almost my fourth year of art. My wife had graduated from Ohio State, and she got her master's degree in art. So we met and she said,

"Take a look at your art."

I took a look at my art actually. I also took a tin of turpentine [makes a hand gesture as if to drink a bottle]. Always makes the art look a little different. And she said,

"You gotta pass on art. You gotta get some other way to go. Because it's not happening on canvas, watercolors, clay, I don't care you know, forget it. You have to do something else."

Well, that kinda put me in a corner and she said,

"There's a watch that they're giving away at the Colonial Theater" [referring to a talent contest in which first place was a wristwatch].

This is in Dayton. I went down, got the watch, got on the air, had no experience with radio other than my mother. I mean I didn't, I wasn't a performer. The guy said,

"All you have to do is time and temperature."

About the second week, you get a little tired of time and temperature. So I started to interview myself. I couldn't get any guests, so I make 'em up, what the hell.

"Here is Monsieur Claude Deauscher. And you're here in Dayton, Ohio. And you're here at the Dayton Art Institute and showing your paintings."

"Yes, wei monse tik shau bairdi" [French gibberish].

"You're gonna have to speak English. This is Dayton."

"Eee, eh, I love Dayton. It's most fascinating city outside of Paris I have ever been in my entire life. I have been to Madrid, I've been to New York, I have been to San Francisco, I have been to Indonesia, I lived on a plantation in Colombia, South America, but Dayton, Ohio, oh, oh, my gosh, me monte wei sonte vere" [French gibberish].

Well, the damn manager ran up the stairs, said,

"Who is that there talking to that frog? What's he doing on the air?"

First off, don't call him a frog, ha, ha. But I was asked to go back to time and temperature. And I went back to it quickly. I had about a year on radio, and I think it was barely a year when my wife Aileen said,

"I'm pregnant! You better go for a raise or go to television, or something else. There's no money in radio, we're gonna have a child."

Oh, oh. So I raced home, my son was born in 1950. Television had just come into Ohio. They had sets, but, of course, nothing worked. It just, it looked like it worked, you know. We made believe, we painted little [gesturing a small picture frame, referring that they painted on their television sets].

I went to Columbus, it was the longest job I had ever had, two-and-a-half years. WBNS stands for wolfs, banks, news, and shoes. I got up to $125 dollars; I started at $75. It sounds like a lot of money, but when your living in a housing project, and one car, and the lawn is just sand, umm, it's depressing.

And so I went in for a five-dollar raise. And the man at the time, of course, everybody is like this when you go in for a raise. I went in for a five-dollar raise, not fifty, but five.

"We brought you on at a time when you had talent, but you were able to hone that knife as it were, hone that talent. You've done very well here, considering. And we don't have the raise."

"Well, that's too bad, because I'm gonna leave here."

"Well, good luck."

Another warm person in my life.

"I'm going to New York."

"What are you going to do there?"

"Look for the monkey on the building."

So, and, of course, the dummy said,

"What monkey?"

"Kong" [chuckles].

At any rate, I went to New York. My wife went to work. And she was dressing mannequins at a department store in Dayton. And our little boy stayed there in Dayton with her. It took me almost six, almost close to seven months, and I brought my wife along with my boy. And the great thing, from this, is we spent eleven years in New York, and out here the rest of the time. But had it not been for that lady, this wife of mine, Aileen, I would've been shot down. I know a lot of guys get carried away, a lot of women, who are great actresses, great talent, great comedians, and forget somehow to give credit to that person who stayed behind. But she backed me all the way.

And I went to New York with $56.46. And I remember I took the bulk of my money and put it in my shoe, because in going to school I'd been rolled constantly. They could never find my money. But I was beaten up a lot and, eventually, I finally got in shape to beat the other guy up—for his money. But at any rate, I didn't wanna tell you that, that's true. My art, I never left my art. I wanted to be an artist, and I'm still trying today and selling a few things. A woman came up to me the other day and I was working in the studio. I'm doing a lot of acrylic work recently, now I say more recently working in penciled drawing, colored pencil, and ink on eight by tens, and heavy paper and stuff. And she came up and she said—it's fun to get the comments from people, even if you don't make a cent, it sounds very sick you know, somewhat ill. You have to have a somewhat warped sense of humor to understand this person who is playing games with you. And she said,

"Uh, Jonathan."

You can tell by the voice [he gestured thumbs down].

"Jonathan, how much is that?"

"That's $15,000."

"Oh, my god—Oh, my god"

"Well, apparently, he's put you on hold. If that's the problem, the next one is $10,150. That's $10,000, and the drawings are $900" [gestures the shape of a small frame].

"I never dreamed they were that much."

"I guess, well, your dream [chuckles] *has come true. And my dream hasn't happened at all."*

Well I said,

"Let me tell you something, sweetheart. These things still take pretty good pictures [points to his eyes]. *Down below you're driving in a Lexus. That's 75 big ones. And your ring would bring in a Delta flight. That's 150. You must have done funny tricks on junior* [points behind him]. *And the shoes are Ferragamo. Okay, how am I doing? And the little watch here is Patek-Philippe. You've got a quarter of a million dollars. and you're playing with me"* [does a hand job gesture]."

Not good. Now, I said,

"You're better off to go to Mexico, Tijuana, and get something on velvet. Sure, get Elvis, guitar. Fifty bucks, everything."

But then I got the lecture, and she said,

"Well, if you weren't Jonathan Winters, you couldn't ask these kinds of prices."

And I said,

"Yes, but I am Jonathan Winters."

[Host walks on stage and presents Jonathan with one of his own paintings.]

"Since we're talking about art, a friend of yours backstage, Jack Riley, gave me a piece, that's one of yours?"

"I hope it is."

"Well now, you can say you've had a show at the Getty.

"Yeah."

"Well show it to the Getty" [host motions outward with his hand].

"You know, it's interesting just what you said, you can now tell them you had a show at the Getty, and, of course, I'll tell them it was in the auditorium, and they'll say, where were the other paintings? You see there are no other paintings, right? So tell them something other than, when you say, you can tell them you had a show at the Getty, be a little more specific. I'll give you some money backstage. See this is my kind of work, and it's different as you can tell" [holds up painting].

"People say to me, 'What are you on?'"

"Ha ha. A roll. I just paint out of my gourd. I do what I can, and a lot of it is—I don't know what's going on."

"A woman asked me the other day,"

"What's going on" [referring to the painting]?

"Well, 36, 19, 7, 25—it's a number painting" [points to the painting].

"How could you tell?"

"Well, I painted over it" [hands painting back to host].

"Where's Uncle Jack?"

"That's all I've got," says the host.

"Is that all you've got? Is it over?"

"It is, Jonathan."

"Where's Jack?"

"He's backstage, waiting for you to go backstage."

"Oh, he's waiting for me? I cheated Jack? Jack, come on—he can come out, can he?"

"He's feeling shy. Jack, do you want to come out for just a moment? Ladies and gentlemen, Jack Riley."

"We're a couple of old guys. Thanks, thanks a lot."

"Jack came all the way from Cleveland, so if he were backstage, he'd be PO'd."

"Ha, ha, true. And I also have some bad news; my audition is not going to go through for Riverdance [referring to his walking with a cane]. *I don't know what to do. Incidentally, they made fun of a guy yesterday because he wore a tie. We go to this MIT shop on Wilshire Boulevard, the both of us* [pointing to his and Jonathan's ties]. *Yes, you're wearing a tie, Jon."*

"I'm wearing roosters."

"So everybody up in Santa Barbara is missing you, I just found out. Some of your favorites that come up to you on the streets."

"No, there's no favorites up there. Just my family."

"Just your family," says Jack Riley.

*"Yeah, I'm after **their** money."*

"The guy, one guy told me, one guy told you that you're nothing but a has-been."

"That's right, but I'm an international has-been."

"That's it."

"That guy is just a local has-been. No, one of my favorites, I told this to Jack backstage. Because we all get this, regardless of what field you may be in. A person will say, a man or a women, will say, especially if you have some semblance of a naughty background, not evil just a little bit naughty,"

"Well, John, I've heard a lot of stories about you."

"Always agree with them."

"Yes, they're all true. Incidentally I've heard nothing about you."

"Okay, well, see you buddy."

"Jonathan Winters, everybody. And Michael Holly" [referring to the host].

"Thank you, thank you for coming."

●   ●   **End Speech**   ●   ●

8

Frank Kern

Speaker: Frank Kern (Online Internet Marketer)

Date: December 27, 2012

Name: How Did Marketing Online Get Started?

Who Created It?

Frank Kern, Monologue Interview

● ● **Key Points** ● ●

Say what you want about Frank Kern. Businessman, con artist, or marketing genius, he is clearly a salesman first and foremost. Unlike Kevin Plank, who focused on providing a unique product to a niche market, Kern uses psychology to sell anything, mostly information and knowledge, to anyone who is willing to listen to him. Plank created a unique product out of his passion for athletics and football. He turned his passions into a successful business in which his livelihood and passions are aligned.

Kern is arguably on the opposite spectrum of Plank. Although both are salesmen, Kern was obviously born naturally with the ability, while Plank grew into it. Kern seems disconnected with whatever his passions are. We know that Plank is passionate about sports and football and his success at Under Armour drives that. But what is Kern really passionate about? Honestly, I'm not sure.

Reviewing currently available information on Kern, you'll find that he's always *"on"* and *"selling."* I think that if there's ever a time Kern isn't selling something, then something must be off the mark. Kern just seems like he enjoys living the life of a retired person, relaxing, driving his fancy cars; living the life of leisure. That is to say, there's nothing wrong with that concept. Some people know what their passions are and find them early on, while others don't know theirs or find theirs later in life. But it seems for Kern that his success, while plentiful, is just a misused resource being spent on cheap frills and desires.

The best interview Kern did, in my opinion, was a monologue in a video posted on the Internet in 2012. His monologue was an obvious sales pitch to "build his brand," but it offers a window into his mindset and his background.

In his monologue, Kern explains the key distinction between someone like himself and Plank. And both Plank and Kern illustrate an example of someone, Plank, who has their livelihood aligned with their passions, someone who enjoys their line of work, because it ties directly to their goals and passions; versus someone like Kern who has a skill that allows them to make a great livelihood, but that skill is misaligned because what they do for a living is not their passion. They are disconnected from their passions, because their line of work is not related to their ultimate goals and passions.

Obviously, we can see that Kern has a gift for public speaking and is an incredible salesman. But he really doesn't have anything behind him; he doesn't seem to have a larger passion or goal. He's just a normal person who wants the finer things in life and wants to get them with the least amount of work possible. And for Kern, it's his ability to sell that gets him these things.

Most of what Kern does is sell, and what he's selling is often up for debate. For some time, it was unclear whether the practices he was engaged in were actually legal. However, this perception was cleared up in November 2003 when Irwin Frank Kern IV, his full name, was sued and ultimately settled with the Federal Trade Commission (FTC) for making false or misleading income claims about the *"pre-package Internet businesses"* he was selling.

Unlike Plank, who focused on providing a unique product to a niche market, Kern uses his persona and psychology to sell his products and services to anyone who is willing to listen to him. Plank created a unique product out of his passion for athletics and football. He turned his passions into a successful business in which his livelihood and passions are aligned. Kern just uses his sales ability to achieve his end goals of fancy cars and luxury living. One could argue that in Kern's mind, his ends justify his means, in that he'll sell anything to get what he wants.

Kern hails from rural Macon, Georgia. He claims that before turning to the Internet to make money he *"never had a job, never had a job more than like six months."* Eventually, he became the manager of a used car lot before opening up his own used car lot, which he claims he *"ran it straight into the ground."* But other than these few factoids, not much is known about Kern and his background.

What you'll mostly find about Kern is the image he portrays online, one of a successful Internet businessman and marketing guru. Which in some aspects is true, but just keep in mind he's always selling you something, and his image is just another part of his tactics. It's things like this that make Kern interesting. Examining the story of a self-taught Internet marketer bring some basic lessons of success to light.

While Kern is unconventional and doesn't hold back on his use of language, he always gets right to the point. Being blunt, he explains that everyone needs to sell. A brilliant engineer who creates a unique invention needs to be able to convince people that his invention is the next best thing, that his invention is a better mousetrap than what's already available. What good would his invention be, if he were unable to even get it out to the public, because of his inability to get others on his team and sell?

It would be similar to the story of the great inventor Nikola Tesla and his struggles to get his inventions funded and sold to the mass market. Tesla, while brilliant was not an outgoing sociable person. One could argue that he was not the best salesman in the room but a great performer at times, giving demonstrations of his alternating current electricity to live audiences across the country. But even his performances couldn't get Tesla the funding he needed.

Tesla's story even brought inspiration for Larry Page, cofounder of Google. Page is quoted as saying that he cried when reading the story of Tesla, because he couldn't stand the fact that great inventions from a brilliant inventor went unpublished and unproduced. Page didn't want another scientist, like Tesla, who had brilliant ideas and inventions to go unheard of again. And Page did just that, becoming a successful young billionaire and going on to fund numerous innovative projects.

Page, himself, could not sell or hold up a room for a speech, yet he surrounded himself with great managers and salespeople, like Eric Schmidt, to sell his ideas to others. Just imagine if Tesla had a talented salesperson like Kern on his side while he was still alive.

This goes back to the idea of specialization and finding your skills and passions. Someone like Kern is a salesman, and a salesman for hire, at that. He is on the sales (PADS) side, and he can take his skills and apply them to almost any product or company he chooses.

People like Tesla or Page are on the STEML side and are uniquely qualified in their respective fields. They can make a livelihood and get by with their skills. But in order to become really successful, they need to learn to sell or get people like Kern on their team to help them sell. This is why the combination of the PADS and STEML quadrants is the most important concept to understand.

Combining a unique skill with sales ability is the perfect combination for success. Whether or not someone's passions or goals are misaligned won't affect the successfulness of their livelihood, if they have a unique skill and the ability to sell. We saw that someone whose passions and livelihood are misaligned, like Kern, is just as successful as someone whose passions and livelihoods are perfectly aligned, like Plank. It all just depends on the quality of life balance you want to achieve.

Regardless of what Kern is selling, there is no doubt that he knows how to sell. His ideas on the ability to sell and his raunchy commentary are thought provoking.

Take a look at Kern's monologue.

Frank Kern
Courtesy: Google Free Images

Narrator (text): Frank Kern: Man, Myth, Legend

Frank Kern: My Name is Frank Kern; I am a salesman, for lack of any other better glamorous description. And I sell things on the Internet. I got into Internet marketing because I got lucky. I was a door-to-door credit card machine salesman. I got tired of the direct, in-person, constant unrelenting rejection. So I went to the Internet in 1999 to figure out how to sell credit card machines, without actually having to talk to somebody.

Somehow, I don't remember how I pulled this off, but I had somehow managed to actually sell a few credit card machines over the Internet. And I don't recall how. I think I did it by just finding like websites and contacting, like literally just calling the people that had the websites and saying, "Hey, you know, you should let me process your credit cards."

So 400 million phone calls later, some dude said yes. Maybe ten guys said yes, or something. And one of the customers I had was a guy in Indiana. And I could see their volume, their transactional volume, every month, you know. And this dude was doing about ten-thousand dollars a month. Which to me was a billion. So I called him. I said, "Man, what are you doin'?"

He said, "Well, I'm sellin' this uh CD-ROM with reports on it."

And I said, "Well how are you sellin' them?"

He goes, "I'm sending SPAM."

And I said, "Will you show me how to do that?"

And he said, "Yeah I will, and every one of these things you sell, I'll give you a little cut of the money." So he showed me how to send SPAM, which you know, from my limited experience, requires whatever degree is right before the rocket science level degree, you've got to have that level of intelligence to send out SPAM.

So I was horrible at it. But it wasn't for lack of effort, you know. But that showed me the power of, if you have a list of people and they actually want to hear from you and you have something that they want in the first place, then you really can make some money. You know, so it was the beginning I guess, the little seedling there that sort of started it all.

Narrator (text): The Internet Lifestyle

Frank Kern: The Internet lifestyle, this mythical Internet lifestyle, you know is perceived as, "Aww, yeah you know, you get up, you do nothing, money comes in, and it's fantastic." Which is, that happens, but if you do that for more than a couple of months, the Internet lifestyle is over. So it's a blessing and a curse. You don't have to do anything, you know what I mean? There is over you, over, you know, no one is cracking the whip, so to speak, saying, "Get to work, let's have at it."

But, other than your customers of course, I mean you do have to deliver on the promises, that's always very inconvenient. You know [chuckles] that gets in the way of the mythological lifestyle. But there's no one, there's no one pushing you, so if you, if you live this Internet lifestyle too long, then you got no more Internet lifestyle and you have to go to work. So that's one aspect of it.

The other aspect of it, which probably most people will tell you, those who are really into this, is the Internet lifestyle really means you're working all the time. You know, I'm eating dinner with the family and like this eye is, this half of the brain is on the conversation [points to his left eye] and this half of the brain is on what are we going to do tomorrow [points to his right eye]. You know, "What are these numbers? What's this opt-in rate percentage looking like? How can we get this up? What's this client's business doing? How can I get this guy more money? How can we help develop this guy back into a product?"

You know, I mean, it never ends. It's on all the time, you know. And that's fun. I wouldn't have that any other way. But the notion of, you know, working a couple of hours a day and getting rich is I don't know anyone who does it, because you just get so hooked on it. You know, I mean there are probably some people that make money and don't really do anything, but I don't know why anyone would want to stop? It's just too much fun.

You know, it's like the Stones [referring to the band the Rolling Stones]. I mean they're a great band; they make great music, why would they stop playing? They're still playing, they don't have to, but they do. You know, and if they did stop, they probably wouldn't be any good anymore, you know.

Narrator (text): Thoughts on the Economy

Frank Kern: So here's my definition of the economy. I think that Person (A) gives Person (B) some money. And in return, Person (B) gives Person (A) something of equal or greater value than the money received. That is the economy; you just take that and multiple that by a billion, that's the economy, right? In my uneducated opinion. With that said, I think its fine.

The trick to it all is to be Person (B) as much as you can, on the receiving end of that money. And the trick to being Person (B) is to find something of equal, or preferably, greater value that you can give to all the Person (A)s out there. And the trick to finding the Person (A) is just to look online or just watch the news or read magazines and seeing what's being sold, you know.

You say, "Oh, man, people are buying the shit out of the Snuggie [popular body-length sleeved-blanket from 2008-2009], maybe I'll make a Super-Snuggie, you know." And they're advertising on the TV, and so I'll advertise on the TV, and I'll just do a better job.

It's not; it's not hard you know. I think, the economy is great. I wouldn't change it at all. And I think we have this current, "The Economy Is Bad," or whatever.

The economy is not bad, the equation got fucked up. You know, Person (A) was giving Person (B) the money, but Person (B) was giving them a bunch of bullshit. So, of course, the equation is skewed right now. But the money didn't go anywhere. There's still plenty of money. It's not like the aliens came and sucked it up, you know, through their big money vacuum, and they're hiding it. Maybe it's in the vault, where the economy is. Maybe it's in the basement, you know, they don't even wear loincloths in the basement. The nubiles just sit there, and they fan the money, like it's a living entity. Come on, it's fine! It's an illusion! Economy!?!

You know a man's gonna buy—a man wants something, he'll buy it. Period. You know, you see the gigantic satellites on the side of the trailer parks. You know, a guy's got a Lexus, but he can't pay child support. Whatever he wants, he's gonna buy it. That's gonna happen 'til the end of time.

If you're a good salesman, you control the economy, period. And if you can be a good salesman, you can get in front of a lot of people, you can control a lot of the economy. You know, and that's the name of the game. And that's all there is to it. Everything else is just guys on TV, trying to scare you into watching their shows, so they can sell advertising crafted by people like me, ha, ha, ha [laughs]. That's really the truth, you know.

Narrator (text): What Is Success?

Frank Kern: I guess you have to consider someone's definition of success, you know. Really umm, when I first started, my dream was $10,000 a month. If I could just make $10,000 a month, I would make more than my teachers or something, you know what I mean. And I never did. I went from making none, to my first real month online was $17,000, and then it grew pretty substantially after that. But I guess, if I were to speak for other people, especially for people just getting started, I think the monetary amount would be, whatever it takes to not have to go to work, you know. I think that's probably the common denominator, especially with everybody that's starting out as well. I'm successful if I don't have to have a job anymore, and I can just stay home and sell my wears and services on the inter-webs.

Narrator (text): Keys to Success

Frank Kern: The keys to being successful online are very, very simple. I actually, there are two commandments I have, on how to be successful online. The first commandment is, "Thou shalt not fuck around." The second commandment is, "Thou shalt not be a pussy." And I'll explain. And really, I think if you obey these two commandments, you'll be fine.

So we'll start with, "Thou shalt not fuck around." Most people spend a lot of time reading forums, buying products, and never doing anything, but fucking around, you know. I'll survey customers in my business. I've surveyed customers in client's businesses that are in the same industry, and we'll say, "Well how many of you have a website now?" And 70 percent of them say, "I have no website, I have no business, I have no product," even though they bought everything.

All right well, clearly they're fucking around, because it says so right in every single thing they bought, here's how you get a website. And furthermore, if you wanna know how to build a website, go to YouTube. So, I think that people fuck around because there's no sense of urgency. So I say, "Listen, I want you to imagine this. Imagine that Osama Bin Laden had a machine gun pointed at your family, and he said you got 24 hours to build a website that can collect an email address or I'm pulling the fuckin' trigger."

You know, I know they would figure out how to build a website, and they wouldn't go a forum saying, "Now which course should I buy that shows me how to build a website? Is this guy a scam? What kinda website should I build?" You can go to YouTube or something, type in, "How to build a website," and pick one from some of the thirty something thousand, freely available tutorials and build the damn site.

You know, and when the site didn't come out perfect, they go back to it, and they build—let's say the table wasn't looking right, or the font wasn't right, they go back to YouTube or Google, and say, "How to make font look right." And then, you know, by twenty hours, they'd have the damn thing up and they'd say, "Okay, Osama, I got the website." Okay, good thank you, see you later. And that'd be the problem solved. So they're just fucking around. You know, if you don't fuck around, you'll be successful. Get to work.

The second of the commandments is, "Thou shalt not be a pussy." It's this, they say, "Well what if I don't? What if it doesn't work, you know?" I'm perfectly willing to spend, go into enormous debt, to attend seminar after seminar after seminar and to buy product after product after product and get all of this education. But I'm terrified to spend $100 on a Google AdWords campaign, to try to launch a product off the ground, to try test a market and everything. They're just being pussies. You know, they're afraid of that failure.

So, if you can accept the truth that you're going to fail about 98 percent of the time, but the 2 percent of the time you don't fail, you're probably going to hit these massive oil wells that can reward you for the rest of your life, you'll be okay. But if you're just gonna be a little pussy about everything and not get to work and not get started and get that temporary like crack-cocaine high, from buying the product that makes you feel like you're doing something, and then that wears off and you buy the next thing. If you're gonna do that instead of actually getting to work and doin' somethin' then, you're, you're screwed, you know.

So the secret to Internet success is you know, get to work, don't fuck around, and don't be a pussy. And when you get knocked down, get back up. Because you're gonna get knocked down, period. It's like talkin' to a guy who's gonna be a boxer. You know, listen, the guy's like, "I wanna be a champion boxer. I'm not gonna get hit am I?"

"Oh no dude, you're not gonna. You're gonna be fine, you're not gonna get hit."

The guy gets hit one time, "I don't wanna be a boxer anymore." Of course, he's never gonna make it as a boxer. He's just gotta know that you're gonna get the shit beat out of you, you know, a lot. And then sometimes you're gonna win, and when you win, you're gonna be on TV, it's gonna be great. Nike is going to call you, and you can have a boxing shoe or something. Maybe Kern will do the ad campaign for you [referring to himself]. Tell America that they'll be beautiful if they wear your boxing shoe, you'll sell millions, you're gonna be fine. But you're gonna get your ass beat, a lot. And that's the trick to it all.

Narrator (text): The Lesson in Failure

Frank Kern: Ha, ha [laughs]. The failures I've encountered. Well this could be a box-set video, you know. We could go on. Well, every business I had, before getting online, and several online ventures, I ran straight into the ground. So I've never had a job, never had a job more than like six months. I was fired from many. I never had a decent respectable job. The closest thing to a respectable job I got, where I was a manager of a car lot. And that's really just a glorified car salesman, not to disrespect the car-selling profession at all. That's very hard work. The men and women who can do that work their asses off, you know. I failed at that, did terrible. I had a little used car lot of my own, ran it straight into the ground. I had a dog-fencing business, straight into the ground.

My first two years I spent as a spammer, I spent all the money I had, you know. And I was a spammer. So not only did I not really make any money, I was also like one of the most hated species of people on the planet, you know. So then the prestige my family, was so proud [chuckles].

"What does your son do?"

"Well, he's a spammer."

"Oh, my goodness, how did he know I had this erectile dysfunction problem? He keeps sending me these Viagra ads."

"No, that's not him, that's his friends. He's the one with the get-rich-quick ads."

Oh yes, of course, you know. So there was that.

My most notorious failure was when I was sued by the Federal Trade Commission (FTC) for my very first product that I created myself, that I called Instant Internet Empires. And man, I thought I was onto something. But apparently they did not think I was onto something at all, you know.

They said, "Well, Mr. Kern, this is a pyramid scheme."

And I said, "What exactly is a pyramid scheme?"

And they said, "Well it looks conspicuously like this program of yours."

You know, I said, "Man, what are we going to do?"

And they said, "Well, I'll tell you what you're going to do. You're going to send out this public message that says we have sued you and seized your assets. And then we're going to take all your money. What do you have to say about that?"

And I said, "Well, okay" [chuckles]. What else are you going to say? I was like, all right, sorry.

You know, so that was a pretty significant failure. That was very embarrassing. I wouldn't trade it for anything, you know. I learned a lot from that process. I certainly would never want to repeat it, wouldn't want to go through it again. But I wouldn't take it back for all the money in the world.

Narrator (text): Reasons for Failure

Frank Kern: So the biggest reason people fail online is twofold. One, the insidious killer of them all, is that they don't get started or they don't get back up. So they get paralyzed with fear, what if this doesn't work. So that takes out 90 percent of them. And then the 9 percent left over will actually try. And it's not going to work out the first time and then they never try again. So that's the biggest killer right there.

The second biggest killer is people never learn how to sell. Most people cannot sell their way out of a paper bag. They get wrapped up in the technology, you know. The get wrapped up in Twitter or Facebook or something. How do I like—they'll go buy a tool that gets them like 9 billion Twitter followers, but they never learn how to sell those people anything. So I'd rather be able to sell ten guys something, than get, you know, 10,000 followers on Twitter or have the flashiest video player or something.

If you learn how to sell, I mean you give me a notepad and a pencil, then I'll write a damn sales letter and hand it out on the street corner, and I'll have $10,000 by tomorrow, you know. Maybe more. Shit, take that away and give me a telephone. Take the telephone away, give me some shoes and drop me off in a neighborhood, and give me anything to sell and god damn it, I will sell it. You know, I might not sell it elegantly.

But if you can sell something, you're set. Forever. If you have that ability, you don't even have to be good. Ninety percent of being able to sell something is being able to put up with the "no." You know, if you can just say, "No? Okay good, thank you, bye." And keep going to the next one, you're fine. So inability to sell and just spinelessness are really the two killers. That's what causes the failure, for sure.

Narrator (text): Teaching Success

Frank Kern: My cousin, who's like a little brother to me, was working as a commercial realtor. And he had finally had enough. You know, I had been after him. We both lived in Macon, Georgia, and I didn't have anyone to hang out with. You know, because I'm at/in my little office all day doing Internet work and I didn't really have to work all the time. Sometimes I wanted to screw off, and everyone else had a job, and I was kinda, you know, I was fucked.

So I was after him, I was like, "Look, man, you gotta get into this, you know. You gotta do this Internet thing. Just try it out."

He says, "No, no, no, I'm gonna be a respectable person."

And I was like, "First of all, you're never going to be a respectable person because you're not one. Neither am I, we're not going to fool anybody; you might as well embrace it."

So finally he'd had enough. And he said, "You know, I, I'm, show me what you do." So he came into my office, I'll never forget this, and he was like, "What do I do? I got this product idea, how do I market it?"

And I said, "First of all, you're going about it backwards. You never ever start with the product. It always starts with the market. And there's three fundamental, you know, characteristics of a market that you look for. They've got to be an irrationally passionate, great in numbers, and easily reached. And the biggest thing is irrationally passionate. You want people who buy stuff all the time."

I used to have this long, drawn-out process on how to find them. And he really helped me shorten that. So he figured out how to reverse engineer, you know, how to find the market. And it's simple. There's a website called ClickBank that everybody watching this probably knows about. And through some stroke of great fortune for the rest of us, ClickBank has gotten their vendors to agree to be featured in this market place, which allows you to sort, by category, who's selling the most stuff. Which is fabulous!

And then they'll tell you how many of their sales come from affiliates. Which basically lets you almost completely reverse engineer somebody's business, you know. So my tip would be to go to that site, pick a category, anyone you want to. And sort that by the top sellers, and see who's selling the most stuff. And then you know you've got a group of buyers. You got empirical proven data. You know if this guy's buying or selling, the number one guy in the sports and fitness category, and he's selling a thing on your golf swing, you know, unequivocally that there's a market there for that. And you know they're buying this particular thing.

So all you've got to do is go into that market, do a better job of selling. And sell a better product, shit, you don't even have to sell a better product, it's just best if you do. So, in all honesty, you just have to do a better job of marketing and selling, and then you can exceed his numbers, which are right there, they're clearly visible for everyone to see. So that's the biggest tip. You can reverse engineer anything. Never, ever, ever, ever, try to reinvent the wheel. You know, don't be the pioneer with the arrows in your back.

Go; use all this unbelievable data that the Internet gives us. Reverse engineer a competitor, and just go in there and take over.

That's what he did. He did it in the hypnosis market. Had a product created. I remember his first—he did his launch. You know, he had run ads on Google AdWords and stuff. Just like we talked about earlier, with the launch. He offered to give things away to get the opt-in list. Finally does the launch. He had a little tiny list, you know like 3,000 people. Finally does the launch, and he goes, "All right I'm gonna launch this thing to my 3,000-person list, you know. Let's sit here and watch it."

And I was like, I knew it was going to be anticlimactic, with that small of a group of people. I said, "Let's go to lunch and then we'll come back and see what happens."

So we go to lunch to Zaxby's Chicken, in Macon, Georgia, on Spring Street, I believe it was. It used to be the Arby's, for all you Georgia people. So we go to lunch there. The little fucker brings his BlackBerry, you know. So he's checking stats. While we're at lunch, he made $300. And this was like, unbelievable, you know. He was like, "Holy crap, I made $300 bucks."

By the end of the day, he'd made $800 and I think the first week he made a couple grand. Within the first forty-eight months, he made over $2.8 million. Yeah, you know. And it was the same formula. And he sold hypnosis and he sold software. Not any—no get-rich-quick stuff, nothing, you know. And it's all based on that.

You find the market first, you find that hungry market. You find out what they want. And then you give it to them. And you give it to them better than the other guy. You know, and if you can do that, you're done. You're unstoppable.

•   •   **End Interview**   •   •

9

Tony Robbins

Speaker: Anthony (Tony) Robbins

Date: January 16, 2007

Name: Tony Robbins—TED Talk

"Why We Do What We Do"

• • **Key Points** • •

And then there was Tony Robbins. What is there to say about Tony Robbins that hasn't already been said? Out of the four examples I've covered, his background is probably the most written about and researched out of all of them. This is in part because Robbins relies heavily on and uses his background and stories from his early childhood to make his livelihood. It's a part of this package he projects, his appeal, when he conducts conferences and performances.

His main use for his background is to show audiences that he literally came from nothing and with hard work and determination he became a successful speaker.

And, according to Robbins, he literally did come from a rough background. He grew up on the outskirts of Los Angeles. His mother and father divorced when Robbins was only seven years old. He first lived with his father, but then at the age of nine moved back in with his mother. Never having enough money he and his family struggled financially.

Robbins eventually found his passion in sports writing, first writing for his high school newspaper and then professionally for his local city newspaper, the *Glendora Press.* Robbins ultimately achieved his dreams of being a local television station reporter. But his unstable family life would crush his dreams at an early age. His abusive mother forbade him from continuing to work as a reporter and demanded that he stop writing to help her out at home. And Robbins had no choice, because even at a young age his mother depended on him and his siblings to do everything from making her meals to doing the laundry.

Robbins' family and financial struggles ultimately forced him to strike out on his own and ultimately gave him the motivation to apply for a sales position selling subscriptions door-to-door, and then eventually starting his own motivational seminar career with Jim Rohn, and the rest is history. He went on to give seminars all around the world.

The thing you'll notice about Robbins is that he is very consistent in his message. Reading and watching him, you'll notice that he has the same pitch, more or less, just in different lengths and amounts. He can give his entire pitch in an hour or he can stretch it out over a week, that's how much material he literally has.

This is evident in Robbins famous TED talk in 2007. His TED talk is probably the best summary of his entire philosophy and mantra. While Robbins has done countless interviews, his TED talk is a great example of the seminar material that he pitches to his thousands of paying followers.

But Robbins is always coming from the point of the finish line, in that he presents himself as a self-made success. He always reminds everyone that *"he's made it,"* and that *"he's very successful."* And there's nothing wrong with this tactic, it's powerful and establishes legitimacy with the audience. I believe it's up to the audience members to actually define what success means to them, but if you think calling yourself successful actually makes you successful, then more power to you.

And I think this where there might be a disconnect between Robbins and his audiences in general. People probably don't actually listen to his advice. He always, clearly states, that he does not teach the *"science of achievement."* As mentioned earlier, Robbins is always coming from the point that he and his audiences are already successful. His assumptions are that his audiences are already successful people, and that they know *"how to take the invisible and make it visible."*

Instead, what Robbins focuses on is what he calls the *"art of fulfillment."* Notice how Robbins coyly distinguishes between *"science"* and *"art,"* claiming that everyone can master science, you just need to study the patterns and *"follow the code."* But this is where I always stop and ask, really? Right here is where most people will keep reading or listening, thinking that the rest of his speech will apply to their efforts in trying to become successful in the first place.

I always took a pause at this juncture in Robbins' speeches because I wanted to know how come he never seems to address the mechanics behind becoming successful. And ultimately this fact and others led me to write this book about how to make a livelihood and be successful at it.

What people see in Robbins is that he'll teach them how they can become successful. But in reality, he teaches from the point of view of someone who is misaligned in their skills and how they make their livelihood. Robbins is assuming, and accurately so, that most people who have a skill are making a living with it, but not everyone is passionate or has found their passion in their livelihood. This would be someone like Frank Kern, who has a skill, but uses it to achieve his other unrelated passions, because what he does with his skill to make a living is not his ultimate goal or passion; unlike Kevin Plank, whose skill and livelihood are aligned with his passion.

Because most people naturally fall into the misalignment category, which is totally fine, because ultimately it's an issue of people's ability to change their quality of life, Robbins focuses on trying to bring people into the alignment category, what many people call self-actualization.

If anything, Robbins offers concepts to try to help people become as closely aligned with their skills and passions as much as possible, because as he says, it's the notion of **"contributing to society"** and **"giving back"** that actually fulfills most people. And again, Robbins' statements on this are true. Simply put, the reason most people are philanthropic and give is because of altruism, it makes them feel good, and people tend do things that benefit them. In an ironic way, giving someone else a gift or charity tends to make the giver feel good.

But I harken back to my original point in that, how do you even become successful enough to contribute and start you own foundations to give back and feel good as Robbins likes to claim?

We covered most of that answer, as it lies within the pages of this book. But Robbins does offer something to help understand how to find your skill in the first place. He says that the **"The defining factor in success is never resources, its resourcefulness."** This is a key aspect to all points on the four quadrants and in both the STEML and PADS categories.

What Robbins is getting at with that statement is that people can always come up with excuses for why they failed at something. It's always something, such as, ***"they didn't have enough time, enough money, enough technology."*** But not having enough resources is not the ***"defining factor,"*** as Robbins claims. He says its emotion, ***"if we get the right emotion, we can get ourselves to do anything. We can get through it. If you're creative enough, playful enough, fun enough, you can get through to anybody,"*** and ***"if you don't have the money, but you're creative enough or determined enough, you find the way. So this is the ultimate resource."***

I believe that it's this simple key that people often overlook. And it's important to understand that your success comes from within, it comes from you. It's difficult at a young age to understand what your skills are and what you might be good at. But the earlier you find your niche, the sooner you can start figuring out how to align your skills with how you make your livelihood.

Anyone from any of the four quadrants can be successful in making a livelihood. It's just the degree of ***"satisfaction"*** or ***"fulfillment"*** that might vary from alignment or misalignment with your passions and goals that can make a difference in determining your quality of life.

As we discussed, the quality of life of someone who has aligned their skills with their passions and goals is quite higher than someone who is using their skill to make a livelihood only to pursue their passions and goals on the side. And we know that the most common method of someone in misalignment to transform into alignment is to make enough money with their skills in order to enjoy and pursue their goals and passions, until the money runs out or until they can actually make it big with the passions and turn it into a skill.

Regardless of your opinion of Robbins, his story-telling skills are remarkable. He has skillfully translated ideas of simple human characteristics into a successful speech and advice-giving livelihood for himself.

Take a look at Tony's speech.

Tony Robbins
Courtesy: Google Free Images

Thank you. I have to tell you that I am both challenged and excited. My excitement is that I get a chance to give something back, my challenge is, the shortest seminar that I usually do is 50 hours. I'm not exaggerating, I do weekends, and what I do, and I do more than that obviously, coach people, but I'm into immersion. Because how did you learn language? You didn't learn it by just learning principles. You got in it, and you did it so often that it became real. And the bottom line of why I'm here, besides being a crazy mofo, is that, I'm really in a position, I'm not here to motivate you obviously, you don't need that. And a lot of times that's what people think I do. And it's the furthest thing from it.

What happens though is, people say to me, "I don't need any motivation," and I say that's interesting that's not what I do. I'm the "why" guy. I want to know why you do what you do. What is your motive for action? What is it that drives you in your life, today? Not ten years ago, or are you running the same pattern? Because I believe that the invisible force of internal drive, activated, is the most important thing in the world. I'm here because I believe emotion is the force of life.

All of us here have great minds. You know most of us here have great minds, right? I don't know if I'm in that category, but we all know how to think, with our minds we can rationalize anything, we can make anything happen. We can, I agree with what was described a few days ago, about this idea that people work in their self-interest. But we all know that notion is bullshit at times. You don't work in your self-interest all the time. Because when emotion comes into it, the wiring in our mind changes, and the way it functions changes.

And so it's wonderful for us to think intellectually about how the life of the world is and especially those who are very smart. We can play this game in our heads, but I really want to know is, what's driving you? And what I'd like to maybe invite you to do by the end of this talk is explore where you are today for two reasons:

1.   So that you can contribute more.

2.   So that hopefully we cannot just understand other people more, but maybe appreciate them more and create the kinds of connections that can stop some of the challenges that we face in our society today, that are only going to get magnified by the very technology that is connecting us.

Because technology is making us intersect. And that intersection doesn't always create the view of "everybody now understand everybody," and "everybody appreciates everybody."

So I've had an obsession basically for 30 years. And that obsession has been, "What makes the difference in the quality of people's lives?" What makes the difference in their performance, because that's what I get hired to do. I got to produce the result now. That's what I've done for 30 years.

I get the phone call when the athlete is burning down on national television and they were ahead by five strokes and now they can't get back on the course. And I have to do something right now and get the result or nothing matters.

I get the phone call when the child is going to commit suicide, and I got to do something right now. And in 29 years I'm very grateful to tell you that I never lost one in 29 years. It doesn't mean I won't someday, but I haven't done it. And the reason is in the understanding of these human needs that I want to talk to you about.

So when I get those calls about performance, that's one thing, like how do you make a change? But also, I'm looking to see what is it that's shaping that person's ability to contribute? To do something beyond themselves. So maybe the real question is, you know, I look at life and can say there is two master lessons:

1. The science of achievement. Which almost everyone in this room has mastered to an amazing extent. That's how do you take the invisible and make it visible, right? How do you take what you're dreaming of and make it happen. Whether it be your business, your contribution to society, money, whatever is it for you, your body, your family.

2. But the other lesson of life that is rarely mastered is the art of fulfillment. Because science is easy, right? We know the rules, you write the code, you follow and you get the result. Once you know the game, you just, you know up the ante, don't you? But when it comes to fulfillment, that's an art. And the reason is, because it's about appreciation and it's about contribution. You can only feel so much by yourself.

So I've had an interesting laboratory where I try to answer the question of, the real question, which is, "What's the difference in somebody's life if you look at somebody like, those people that you've given everything to, like all the resources they say they need?" You gave them not a hundred-dollar computer; you gave them the best computer. You gave them love, you gave them joy, you were there to comfort them.

And those people very often, and you know some of them I'm sure, end up the rest of their life with all this love, education, money, and background, spending their life going in and out of rehab. And then you meet people that have been through ultimate pain—psychologically, sexually, spiritually, emotionally abused. And not always, but often they become some of the people that contribute the most to society.

So the question we've got to ask ourselves really is, "What is it? What is it that shapes us?" And we live in a therapy culture. Most of us don't do that, but the culture is a therapy culture. And what I mean by that is the mindset that we are our past. And everybody in this room, you wouldn't be in this room if you bought that theory, but most of society thinks that biography is destiny. The past equals the future. And, of course, it does if you live there. But what people in this room know, and what we have to remind ourselves though, because you can know something intellectually, you can know what to do and then not use it, not apply it. So really what we have to remind ourselves is that decision is the ultimate power. That's what it really is.

Now when you ask people, you know, "Have you failed to achieve something?" How many have ever failed to achieve something significant in your life say, "I," thanks for the interaction on a high level there. But if you ask people why didn't you achieve something. Somebody who is working for you, you know, or a partner, or even yourself. When you fail to achieve a goal, what's the reason people say they failed to achieve. What do they tell you? Don't have the—Didn't know enough. Didn't have the knowledge. Didn't have the money. Didn't have the time. Didn't have the technology. I didn't have the right manager. Didn't have the Supreme Court.

And, and what do all those, including the Supreme Court, have in common? They are a claim to your missing resources. And they may be accurate. You may not have the money; you may not have the Supreme Court. But that is not the defining factor. And you correct me if I'm wrong. The defining factor is never resources, its resourcefulness. And what I mean specifically, rather than just some phrase, is if you have emotion, human emotion.

Something that I experienced from you [referring to Vice President Al Gore who lost the 2004 elections], the day before yesterday at a level that is as profound as I've ever experienced, and if you communicated with that emotion I believe you would have beat his ass and won. But how easy for me to tell him what he should do. "Idiot Robbins."

But I know, when we watched the debates, when we watched the debate at that time, there were emotions that blocked people's ability to get to this man's intellect and capacity, in the way that he came across to some people in that day. Because I know people that want to vote in your direction and didn't, and I was upset. But there was emotion that was there.

How many of you know what I'm talking about here say, "I." So emotion is it. If we get the right emotion, we can get ourselves to do anything. We can get through it. If you're creative enough, playful enough, fun enough, can you get through to anybody, yes or no? If you don't have the money, but you're creative enough or determined enough, you find the way.

So this is the ultimate resource. But this is not the story that people tell us. The story that people tell us is a bunch of different stories. They tell us that we don't have the resources, but ultimately if you take a look here. Flip it up if you would. They say what are all the reasons they have in common, we said that. Next one please. He's broken my pattern that son of a bitch [jokingly referring to Vice President Al Gore]. But I appreciate the energy, I'll tell ya' that.

What determines your resources, we've said that decisions shape destiny, which is my focus here. If decisions shape destiny, what determines it is three decisions:

1. What am I going to focus on?

2. What does it mean?

3. What are you going to do?

What are you going to focus on? Right now you have to decide what you are going to focus on. In this second, consciously or unconsciously. The minute you decide to focus on something, you got to give it a meaning. And whatever that meaning is, it produces emotion. Is this the end or the beginning? Is God punishing me or rewarding me? Or is this the roll of the dice? An emotion then creates what we're going to do, or the action.

So think about your own life. The decisions that have shaped your destiny. And that sounds really heavy, but in the last five or ten years or fifteen years, haven't there been some decisions you've made that if you made a different decision, your life would be completely different? How many people can think of one, honestly, better or worse, say "I."

So the bottom line is maybe it was where to go to work and you met the love of your life there. Or maybe it was a career decision. I know the Google genius I saw here, I mean I understand that their decision was to sell their technology at first. What if they made that decision, versus to build their own culture? How would the world be different? How would their lives be different, their impact?

The history of our world is these decisions. When a woman stands up and says, "No, I won't go to the back of the bus" [referring to Rosa Parks in Alabama, in 1955]. She didn't just affect her life, that decision shaped our culture. Or someone standing in front of a tank [referring to Tiananmen Square, China, in 1989].

Or being in a position like Lance Armstrong and someone says to you that you've got testicular cancer. That's pretty tough for any male, especially if you ride a bike. You got it in your brain, you got it in your lungs, but what was his decision on what to focus on? It was different than most people. What did it mean? It wasn't the end, it was the beginning. What am I going to do? He goes off and wins seven championships; he never won once before the cancer, because he got emotional fitness, psychological strength.

That's the difference in human beings that I've seen of the three million that I've been around. Because that's what I've had in my lab. I've had three million people from eighty different countries that I've had a chance to interact with over the last 29 years. And after a while patterns become obvious. You see that South America and Africa may be connected in a certain way, right? Other people say, "Oh, that sounds ridiculous." It's simple.

So what shaped Lance? What shapes you? Two invisible forces.

1. State. We've all had times. Have you ever had a time you did something and after you did it, you thought to yourself, "I can't believe I said that," or "I can't believe I did that, that was so stupid." Who has been there say, "I." Have you ever done something and after you go, "Mmm, mmm, mmm, that was me," [in a gloating tone]. It wasn't your ability, it was your state.

2. Your model of the world is what shapes you long term. Your model of the world is your filter. That is what's shaping us. That's what makes people make decisions.

If you want to know how to influence somebody, you have to know what already influences them. And it's made up of three parts, I believe.

First, what's your target, what are you after? Which I believe it's not your desires. You can get your desires and goals. How many of you have ever got your desire or goal and thought, "Is this all there is?" How many of you have been there say, "I." So it's needs we have. I believe we have six human needs.

Second, once you know what the target that's driving you is, and that you uncover it for the truth, you don't form it, you uncover it.

[**Third**] Then you find out what's your map. What's the belief systems that are telling you how to get those needs? Some people think the way to get those needs is destroy the world. Some people's way is to build something, create something, love someone. And then there is the fuel you pick.

So very quickly six needs. Let me tell you what they are. First one, **certainty**. Now these are not goals or desires. These are universal. Everyone needs certainty that they can avoid pain and at least be comfortable. Now how do you get it? Control everybody, develop a skill, give up, smoke a cigarette. And if you got totally certain ironically, even though we all need that, like if you're not certain about your health or your children or money, you don't think about much more. You're not sure if the ceiling is going to hold up; you're not going to listen to any speaker. But, while we go about getting certainty differently, when we get total certainty, we get what? What do you feel if you're certain? You know what's going to happen, when it's going to happen, how it's going to happen. What would you feel? Bored out of your mind.

So God, in her infinite wisdom, gave us a second human need, which is **uncertainty**. We need variety. We need surprise. How many of you here love surprises, say "I." Bullshit, you like the surprises you want. The ones you don't want, you call problems, but you need them. So variety is important. Have you ever rented a video or a film that you've already seen? Who's done this? Get a fucking life [Tony says jokingly]. Right? Why are you doing it? You're certain it's good because you've read it before, saw it before, but you're hoping it's been long enough you've forgotten if there's variety.

Third human need is critical. **Significance**. We all need to feel important, special, unique. You can get it by making more money. You can do it by getting more spiritual. You can do it by getting yourself in a situation where you put more tattoos and earrings in places humans don't want to know. Whatever it takes. The fastest way to do this, if you have no background, no culture, no belief in resources or resourcefulness, is violence. If I put a gun to your head and I live in the hood, instantly I'm significant, zero to ten, how high? Ten. How certain am I that you are going to respond to me? Ten. How much uncertainty is there? Who knows what's going to happen next? Kind of exciting, like climbing up into a cave and down—that stuff all the way down there is variety and uncertainty.

And it's significant, isn't it? You're willing to risk your life for it. So that's why violence has always been around and will be around, unless we have a consciousness change as a species. Now you can get significance a million ways but in order to be significant you got to be unique and different.

Here's what we really need, **connection and love,** fourth need. We all want it, most people settle for connection because love is too scary. Don't want to get hurt. Who here has ever been hurt in an intimate relationship, say "I." If you don't raise your hand, you'll have that other shit too, come on. And you're going to get hurt again, aren't you glad you came to this positive visit? But here's what's true is that we need it. We can do it through intimacy, through friendship, through prayer, through walking in nature. If nothing else works for you, get a dog. Don't get a cat, get a dog. Because if you leave for two minutes, it's like you've been gone for six months, when you show back up again five minutes later.

Now these four needs everyone finds a way to meet. Even if you lie to yourself, even if you have to have split personalities. But the last two needs, the first four needs are called the needs of the personality, is what I call them.

The last two are the needs of the spirit. And this is where fulfillment comes from. You won't get fulfillment from the first four. You'll figure a way, smoke, drink, do whatever to meet the first four.

But the last two, number five, you must **grow**. We all know the answer here, if you don't grow, you what? If a relationship is not growing, if a business is not growing, if you're not growing, it doesn't matter how much money you have, how many friends you have, how many people love you, you still feel like hell. And the reason we grow, I believe, is so that we have something to give of value.

Because the sixth need is to **contribute** beyond ourselves. Because we all know, corny as it sounds, the secret to living is giving. We all know life is not about me, it's about we. This culture knows that, this room knows that. And it's exciting. When you see Nicholas up here talking about his hundred-dollar computer. The most passionate and exciting thing is that, here is a genius, but he's got a calling now. You can feel the difference in him and it's beautiful. And that calling can touch other people.

In my own life, my life was touched because when I was eleven years old, Thanksgiving, no money, no food, and we're not going to starve, but my father was totally messed up. My mom was letting him know how bad he had messed up. And somebody came to the door and delivered food. My father made three decisions. I know what they were briefly. His focus was, this is charity. What does it mean? I'm worthless. What do I got to do? Leave my family, which he did. At the time it was one of the most painful experiences of my life.

My three decisions gave me a different path. I said focus on; there is food, what a concept. Second, that this is what changed my life; it would shape me as a human being. Somebody's gift, I don't even know who it is, my father always said no one gives a shit. And all the sudden someone I don't even know, they're not asking, they're just giving our family food, looking out for us. It made me believe this, what does it mean? That stranger's care.

And what that made me decide is that if strangers care about me and my family, I care about them. What am I going to do? I'm going to do something to make a difference. So when I was 17, I went out one day, Thanksgiving, it was my target for years to have enough money to feed two families. The most fun thing I ever did in my life, the most moving. Then next year I did four. I didn't tell anybody what I was doing. Next year, eight. I wasn't doing it for brownie points. But after eight, I thought, "Shit, I could use some help."

So sure enough, I went out and what did I do? I got my friends involved and I grew companies, and then I had eleven companies, and then I built a foundation. Now eighteen years later, I'm happy to tell you that last year we fed two million people in thirty-five countries through our foundation, all during the holidays, Thanksgiving, Christmas, in all these different countries around the world. So I don't tell you that to brag, I tell you that because I'm proud of human beings. Because they get excited to contribute, once they've had the chance to experience it and not just talk about it.

So finally, the target that shapes you, here's what's different about people. We have the same needs, but are you a certainty freak, is that what you value most? Or uncertainty? This man here couldn't be a certainty freak if he climbed through those caves. Are you driven by significance or love? We all need all six needs, but whatever your lead system is, it tilts you in a different direction.

And as you move in a direction you have a destination or destiny. The second piece is the map. Think of that as the operating system that tells you how to get there. And some people's map is "I'm going to save lives even if I die for other people," and they're a fireman. Somebody else says that "I'm going to kill people to do it."

They're trying to meet the same needs of significance, right? They want to honor God or honor their family, but they have a different map. And there are seven different beliefs, and I can't go through them because I'm out of time.

But the last piece is emotion. I say that one of the parts in the map is like time. Some people's idea of a long time is 100 years. Somebody else's is ten seconds, which is what I have left for my talk. And the last one, I've already mentioned, if you have a target on your map, and let's say I can't use Google because I love Macs and they haven't made it good for Macs yet, so I use MapQuest. How many have made this fatal mistake of using MapQuest at some time? You use this thing and you don't get there. Well, imagine if your belief system guaranteed that you can never get to where you want to go.

The last thing is emotion. Now here's what I'll tell you about emotion. There are 6,000 words for emotions that we all have words for in the English language. Which is just a linguistic representation, right? It changes by language. But if your dominant emotion, if have more time, I have 20,000 people or 1,000, and I have them write down all the emotions that they experience in an average week. And I gave them as long as they need.

And on one side they write empowering emotions and the other side they write disempowering. Guess how many emotions people experience? Less than twelve. And half of those make them feel like shit. So they got five or six good freaking feelings, right? It's like they feel happy, happy, excited, oh shit, frustrated, frustrated, overwhelmed, depressed. How many of you know somebody who, no matter what happens, finds a way to get pissed off? How many know somebody like this? Or no matter what happens, they find a way to be happy or excited. How many know somebody like this? Come on.

When 9-11 happened, and I'll finish with this, I was in Hawaii. I was with 2,000 people from forty-five countries. We were translating four languages simultaneously for a program I was conducting for a week. The night before was called emotional mastery. I got up had no plan for this, and I said, we had all these fireworks, I do crazy shit, fun stuff, and then at the end I stopped and I had this plan that I was going to say, but I never do what I'm going to say.

126

And all the sudden I said, when do people really start to live? When they face death. And then I went through this whole thing about if you were not going to get off this island, if nine days from now you were going to die, who would you call, what would you say, what would you do? One woman that night is when 9-11 happened.

One woman had come to the seminar, and when she came there, her previous boyfriend had been kidnapped and murdered. Her friend or new boyfriend had wanted to marry her, and she said no. He said, "If you leave me and go to that Hawaii thing, it's over with us." She said, "It's over."

When I finished that night, she called him and left a message, true story, at the top of the World Trade Center where he worked, saying, "Honey, I love you, I just want you to know I want to marry you, it was stupid of me."

She was asleep, because it was 3am for us, when he called her back from the top and said, "Honey, I can't tell you what this means," he said, "I don't know how to tell you this, but you have given me the greatest gift, because I'm going to die."

And she played the recording for us in the room. She was on Larry King later. And he said. "You're probably wondering how on earth this could happen to you twice," and he said, "All I can say to you is this must be God's message to you, honey—from now on every day give your all, love your all. Don't let anything ever stop you."

She finishes and a man stands up, and he says, "I'm from Pakistan, I'm a Muslim, I'd love to hold your hand and say I'm sorry, but frankly this is retribution. I can't tell you the rest because I'm out of time [Tony looks back at the coordinator of the program and is reassured he can finish the story].

Okay, ten seconds. I want to be respectful. All I can tell you is that I brought this man on stage with another man from New York who worked in the World Trade Center, because I had about 200 New Yorkers there. More than 50 lost their entire companies, their friends, marking off their Palm Pilots.

And what I did to people was I said, "What are we going to focus on? What does this mean? And what are we going to do?" I took the group and I got people to focus on, if you didn't lose somebody today, your focus is going to be on how to serve somebody else. There were people, one got up, and she was so angry and screaming and yelling. And I found out that she wasn't from New York, she's not an American, she doesn't know anybody here.

I said, "You always get angry." She said yes. Guilty people felt guilty. Sad people got sad. And I took these two men, and did what I call an indirect negotiation. Jewish man, with family in the occupied territories, from New York, who would have died if he was at work that day. And this man who wanted to be a terrorist, and made it very clear.

The integration that happened is on a film, which I'll be happy to send you, so you can really see what actually happened instead of my verbalization of it. But the two of them not only came together and changed their beliefs and models of the world, but they worked together to bring for almost four years now to various mosques and synagogues the idea of how to create peace. And he wrote a wonderful book, which is called, *My Jihad, My Way of Peace.*

So transformation can happen. My invitation to you is this. Explore your web. The web in here [Tony points to his head]. The needs, the beliefs, the emotions, that are controlling you. For two reasons: So there is more of you to give and achieve too. We all want to do that, but I mean give, because that's what's going to fill you up. And second, so you can appreciate, not just understand, that's intellectual, that's the mind. But appreciate what's driving other people. It's the only way our world is going to change. God bless you. Thank you. I hope this was helpful.

•   •   **End Speech**   •   •

10

Final Thoughts

Essentially it all comes down to you. What's inside **YOU** is what counts the most. This might come off as *"easy"* or *"simple,"* but it's the truth. It's just like the Zac Brown Band quote mentioned in Chapter 5, ***"Life's too easy to be so damn complicated."*** I know you want to, like a lot of things in life, but we don't have to overthink this.

Knowing yourself and understanding your passions, goals, and desires is what will ultimately help you in your journey to match your abilities and skills into making yourself a livelihood that drives your success. And remember this key word, ***"journey."*** Your life won't just magically start after you find your skill. Your journey to discover your passions, goals, and skills is a part of your life, so live it! That first leg of your journey is the road trip to your destination. After you get there, what are you going to do with your passions and skills? *(Hopefully make a livelihood for yourself!)*

This notion might sound repetitive, but it is the one constant that is echoed by nearly almost every successful person I've read about. And if they don't come out and say it directly, like Tony Robbins, then they almost always allude to it, like Kevin Plank.

Many people will say that one's upbringing is important in determining your success. Yes, this is true to an extent. Even things that are out of your control can determine your success, whether you like it or not. You can't control who your parents are or who your siblings are or the amount of resources your family has or lack thereof when you're born.

Yet, for some reason, people can succeed even given the most gruesome of circumstances. Take the **"hand you were dealt with,"** throw it into the dealer's face, leap out of your chair, grab the blackjack table, flip it over, and get the hell out of that addictive casino that is your negative preconceived mindset. I'm a believer in this idea that you can make your own success, because I've seen it time and again. You just have to use what's already inside you.

I'm not arguing that the environment one grows up in or lives in has absolutely no influence on one's success, it certainly does. But the goal here is to recognize a potentially negative environment and run it over like the annoying speed bump that it is and get on with your journey. Don't stop, because it looks like a roadblock.

If your environment is impairing you, then work to change it. If your environment is supporting you, then embrace it. Because you can work to change your surroundings, I don't believe it's the make-or-break factor of your success. There are other factors that have much larger degrees of impact compared to environment.

The chief notion is to know yourself and what's inside of you. Everyone's environment at the beginning is predetermined, we can't choose it. But it's what you do after, that makes a difference.

The fictional character Rocky Balboa, played by Sylvester Stallone, has a famous quote,

> *"You, me or nobody is going to hit as hard as life.*
> *But it ain't about how hard you're hit,*

it is about how hard you can get hit and keep moving forward,
how much can you take and keep moving forward.
That's how winning is done!"

You are born into XYZ family, in XYZ city, with XYZ conditions, and XYZ resources, what are you going to do about it? Are you going to wallow in your sorrows, or set your mind to a goal and find your skill and make a livelihood for yourself?

It's so easy to say, ***"Yeah, I know myself,"*** or ***"I took the time to look inside myself."*** But how many of us actually understand what we know about ourselves? As I've mentioned, our backgrounds and our pasts shape who we are today, but what about our goals, passions, and ambitions? How well do we really know ourselves?

If you can figure yourself out, you've likely succeeded at solving the most difficult puzzle of your life. Because once you know who you are, you can find your passions. Then you can assess your skills and figure out what you're good at and what you might possibly want to learn or get better at. Then you can go out and tackle your goals.

Then comes that sweet success, that point when you have figured out you're actually making a livelihood using your skills and doing what you want to do—what you are passionate about. That is true success.

That's when you've not only brought home the bread and butter, but you actually get to taste that sweet and crunchy bacon, the bacon of success.

References

Baloooba. "Anthony Robbins on A&E Biography FULL Movie." YouTube. 3 June 2013. Web. 27 Oct. 2014. <https://www.youtube.com/watch?v=8ea1TL_vY7g>.

Carlson, Nicholas. "The Untold Story Of Larry Page's Incredible Comeback." *Business Insider*. Business Insider, Inc., 24 Apr. 2014. Web. 25 Apr. 2014. <http://www.businessinsider.com/larry-page-the-untold-story-2014-4>.

Carpenter, Ben. *The Bigs: The Secrets Nobody Tells Students and Young Professionals about How to : Choose a Career, Find a Great Job, Do a Great Job, Be a Leader, Start a Business, Manage Your Money, Stay out of Trouble, Live a Happy Life.* First Edition ed. Wiley, 2014. Print.

EG Conference. "Jonathan Winters at EG 2007." YouTube. The-eg.com, 12 Apr. 2013. Web. 20 Dec. 2014. <https://www.youtube.com/watch?v=SndTc_CLM88>.

Flatley, Joseph L. "Scamworld: 'Get Rich Quick' Schemes Mutate into an Online Monster." *The Verge*. Vox Media, Inc, 10 May 2012. Web. 25 Oct. 2014. <http://www.theverge.com/2012/5/10/2984893/scamworld-get-rich-quick-schemes-mutate-into-an-online-monster>.

Graham, Scott. "The Man behind the 'armour'" *Baltimore Business Journal*. American City Business Journals, 29 Dec. 2003. Web. 25 Oct. 2014.<http://www.bizjournals.com/baltimore/stories/2003/12/29/story4.html>.

Horn, Brian. "Frank Kern's Secret to Success Is Simpler Than Expected." *The Huffington Post*. AOL, Inc, 9 Sept. 2014. Web. 25 Oct. 2014. <http://www.huffingtonpost.com/brian-horn/frank-kerns-secret-to-suc_b_5785006.html>.

Horowitz, Ben. *The Hard Thing about Hard Things: Building a Business When There Are No Easy Answers.* HarperBusiness, 2014. Print.

Kaminski, Vincent. "Risk Managers Should Learn from the Mistakes of Others." *Www.risk.net*. Incisive Risk Information Limited, 12 Mar. 2014. Web. 12 July 2014. <http://www.risk.net/energy-risk/opinion/2330358/risk-managers-should-learn-from-the-mistakes-of-others>.

Kern, Frank. "How Did Marketing Online Got Started? Who Created It? Psychological -Work From Home." YouTube. EmpowerNetworkClub1, 27 Dec. 2012. Web. 17 May 2014. <http://www.youtube.com/watch?v=6P8CH0-kcbM>.

O'Toole, Garson. "Whatever You Are, Try To Be a Good One." Quote Investigator. WordPress, 3 Oct. 2014. Web. 2 Mar. 2015. <http://quoteinvestigator.com/2014/10/03/be-good/>.

Palmisano, Trey. "From Rags to Microfiber: The Story of Under Armour." *SI.com*. Time, Inc, 9 Apr. 2009. Web. 25 Oct. 2014. <http://www.si.com/more-sports/2009/04/09/under-armour>.

Parrish, Shane. "The Difference between Good and Bad Organizations." *Farnam Street*. Farnam Street Media Inc., 20 Jan. 2015. Web. 22 Jan. 2015. <http://www.farnamstreetblog.com/2015/01/ben-horowitz-good-and-bad-organizations/>.

Plank, Kevin. "Grow This House." YouTube. GE Capital, Tom Keene, 7 Nov. 2013. Web. 4 May 2014. <http://www.youtube.com/watch?v=GyuQY8bPySU>.

Robbins, Tony. "Tony Robbins' TED Talk." YouTube. TEDx, 1 Oct. 2012. Web. 13 Apr. 2014. <http://www.youtube.com/watch?v=BwFOwyoH-3g>.

Rose, Charlie. "Steve Ballmer: From Microsoft to LA Clippers." *Bloomberg Business*. Charlie Rose, LLC, 22 Oct. 2014. Web. 23 Oct. 2014. <http://www.bloomberg.com/news/videos/2014-10-22/steve-ballmer-charlie-rose-1022>.

Taleb, Nassim Nicholas. *The Black Swan: The Impact of the Highly Improbable.* Second Ed., Random Trade Pbk. ed. New York: Random House Trade Paperbacks, 2010. Print.

Wagner, Dennis. "In Arizona, Career Channeling Aims to Stem 'disconnect'" *USA Today*. Gannett, 1 Oct. 2014. Web. 17 Dec. 2014. <http://www.usatoday.com/story/news/nation/2014/10/01/career-channeling-aims-stem-training-disconnect/16442061/>.

Thank You

Thank you for reading my book. If you enjoyed it, please take a moment to leave a review.

About the Author

Stevan Pirkovic is a seasoned entrepreneur with a career spanning several fields from finance, retail, politics, and most recently in higher education, with one of the top research universities in the country. Born in Flint, Michigan, Stevan earned his BBA and degree in economics from the University of Michigan-Flint. Stevan currently resides in Ann Arbor, Michigan, and in his spare time serves as a volunteer board member at his local credit union.

Once an avid investor, Stevan earned his Series 3 certification for trading commodities and futures contracts from the National Futures Association (NFA). Stevan still trades the markets but has turned his focus to market research and long-term investment strategies.

An aspiring author, Stevan decided to share his observations about life and the lessons he has learned along the way. His efforts led him to create the ultimate guide on how to successfully make a livelihood. You can connect with Stevan at Stevan@Pirkovic.com.

www.ingramcontent.com/pod-product-compliance
Lightning Source LLC
Chambersburg PA
CBHW061729020426
42331CB00006B/1159